GROWTH FAILURE IN MATERNAL
DEPRIVATION

GROWTH FAILURE IN MATERNAL DEPRIVATION

By

ROBERT GRAY PATTON, M.D.
Department of Pediatrics
Children's Hospital of San Francisco
San Francisco, California

and

LYTT I. GARDNER, M.D.
Professor of Pediatrics
Upstate Medical Center
State University of New York
Syracuse, New York

With an Introduction by

JULIUS B. RICHMOND, M.D.
Professor and Chairman
Upstate Medical Center
State University of New York
Syracuse, New York

4456

WS
105.5
.D3
P322
1963

CHARLES C THOMAS • PUBLISHER
Springfield · Illinois · U.S.A.

Published and Distributed Throughout the World by

CHARLES C THOMAS · PUBLISHER

BANNERSTONE HOUSE

301-327 East Lawrence Avenue, Springfield, Illinois, U.S.A.

*With THOMAS BOOKS careful attention is given to all details of
manufacturing and design. It is the Publisher's desire to present books
that are satisfactory as to their physical qualities and artistic possibilities
and appropriate for their particular use. THOMAS BOOKS will be true
to those laws of quality that assure a good name and good will.*

Printed in the United States of America

TO OUR MOTHERS

Frances Gray Patton
and
Bettie Sue Gardner

Questa condizione, oltre alle già descritte manifestazioni
di carattere psicologico, comprende tutto un corteo di sin-
tomi di ordine somatico: scarso accrescimento pondo-statu-
rale, particolare suscettibilità alle malattie infettive, par-
ticolare gravità delle medesime allorché si determinano.
Che cosa hanno a che fare questi sintomi organici con la
mancanza di cure materne? Per il lattante, più che mai è
evidente come le due istanze, soma e psiche, siano inscindi-
bile e come ciò che gli permette di prosperare fisicamente
gli sia anche necessario stimolo per un buono sviluppo
psichico.

RENATA GADDINI,
Il Bambino, Il Medico, La Medicina,
Ediz. G. Malipiero, Bologna, 1958, p. 120

Introduction

The development of the human newborn infant into an organism with well integrated and differentiated responses and with an emerging personality in the space of relatively few months is a never ending source of wonder to parents and scientific observers alike. This development is conditioned to a considerable extent by man's genetic endowment with a uniquely complex central nervous system which has the potentialities for species-specific and individual-specific responses.

From clinical observation we know that genetic potentialities of the human organism are not expressed unless a complex of stimuli (which we generally call mothering) in a favorable environment come to influence the infant. The precise pattern of stimu-

vii

lation for optimal development has traditionally been defined by the culture. It has been relatively few years since attention was focussed on the significance of the early environment of the child with the publication of the WHO monograph *Maternal Care and Mental Health.*

The interest in this problem in recent years has been sufficiently intense to warrant the publication by the WHO in 1962 of a reassessment of the problem *(Deprivation of Maternal Care: A Reassessment of Its Effects).*[1] That this concern with the relationship of the young human organism and his environment is not a new one among physicians is evident from the following, taken from the writings of Oribasius (A.D. 325-403):

> Infants who have just been weaned should be permitted to live at their ease and enjoy themselves: They should be habituated to repose of the mind and exercise in which little deceptions and gaiety play a part: Their diet should be light in quality and moderate in quantity; for those who, at the period of weaning, stuff them with food and endeavor to give them rich nourishing foods will pervert their nutrition and prevent their growth from the very weakness of their natures. Some of these children will be affected with ulcerations and inflammations of the intestines, with procidentia ani and with grave disease, resulting from the frequency of indigestion and diarrhea. After the sixth or seventh year, little girls and boys should be confided to humane and gentle teachers: for those who attract children to themselves, who employ persuasion and exhortation as a means of instruction and who praise their pupils often, will succeed better with them and will do more to incite their zeal to studies: their instruction will rejoice the children and put them at their ease. Now, relaxation and a joyous spirit contribute much to digestion and favorable nutrition; but those who, on the other hand, are insistent in instruction, who resort to sharp reprimands, will make the children servile and timorous and will inspire them with an aversion for the objects of their instruction. . . .[2]

Thus, the effects of early care on both psychological and biological development were appreciated in relatively sophisticated terms even in ancient times. Although there has been considerable interest in the effects of early sensory deprivation on psychological development in recent years, few systematic studies have been done to elucidate its effects on biological development.

The study reported in this volume is of particular significance, therefore, in throwing some light on the effects of early environment on a basic biological process—growth. That it deals with situations in which the deprivation is rather pronounced renders it no less important. For the history of medical progress is replete with examples in which advances have been initiated with the study of advanced pathology.

This is a pioneering study in that it presents data indicating the impact of sensory deprivation on growth. As is true of pioneering ventures, it presents many challenges for the future. The biological pathways by which environmental circumstances influence basic processes such as growth remain matters for further investigation. Elucidation of these issues is destined to shed further light on the early development of mind-body relationships. And in the process some forward steps will be taken in the direction of man's eternal quest for a deeper understanding of himself and his development.

JULIUS B. RICHMOND, M.D.
Professor and Chairman, Department of Pediatrics
State University of New York, Upstate Medical Center
Syracuse, New York

References

1. *Deprivation of Maternal Care: A Reassessment of Its Effects,* Public Health Papers 14, WHO, Geneva, 1962.
2. Ruhräh, J.: *Pediatrics of the Past.* New York, Hoeber, 1925, p. 13.

Foreword

This book is based on clinical observations made by the authors during their studies of young children with severe retardation of growth and bone maturation. A significant number of these children, having no detectable endocrine or metabolic disorders, were found to have the physical and behavioral characteristics of "anaclitic depression." Study of the environments in each of these cases revealed severe disturbance of family organization, and deprivation of the normal relationships between parents and children. Correction of these factors in hospital and foster home produced improvement in growth rates and in emotional and intellectual development.

It is proposed here that this syndrome represents a truly "psychosomatic" disorder. Although it was impossible to reproduce the exactitude of the laboratory, clinical studies indicated that the growth delay was far out of proportion to the caloric deficits. It is thought, then, that this syndrome exemplifies a more direct effect of emotional illness on intermediary metabolism. Neuroanatomical investigations have shown that the limbic cortex is the "meeting ground" of emotional and metabolic brain functions, and seem to give more substance to our hypothesis.

We believe that this book will be of interest to all physicians who care for children, and especially the pediatrician. The child psychiatrist and the clinical psychologist will find described here the organic manifestations of a syndrome whose behavioral and psychometric aspects they have already studied. The psychiatric social worker and the social agency worker may find these studies useful. Personnel involved in foster home placement endeavors may gain more insight into the complex interaction between the psychological and physiological states of their small patients. Finally, we would hope that scientists in biology and in the basic behavioral sciences might find useful this study of the organic manifestations of a special form of sensory deprivation.

ROBERT GRAY PATTON, M.D.
San Francisco, California
and
LYTT I. GARDNER, M.D.
Syracuse, New York

Acknowledgments

The authors wish to express their appreciation for helpful advice from Doctors Julius B. Richmond, Earle L. Lipton and Leonard Hersher, who have previously studied some of the children described in this monograph with special interest in the behavioral aspects of the syndrome.

Thanks are also due to the case workers of the Children's Division, Onondaga County Department of Public Welfare, Syracuse, New York, for their efforts in overseeing the care of these children, and for their interest and cooperation in the medical follow-up of these cases.

The assistance of the Department of Photography, State University of New York, Upstate Medical Center, is gratefully acknowledged, with special thanks to Mr. Louis Georgianna for his excellent photography. The contribution of the Department of Medical Illustration, Upstate Medical Center, is also noted here with thanks: Mr. Nicholas Apgar designed the title page and dust cover, and Mrs. Julia Hammack skillfully prepared all the charts in this book.

The authors are especially indebted to medical students, Miss Opal Bohall, Miss Angela Diamond, Mr. Bruce Geer, Mr. Don Mayerson, and Mr. Pasqual Perrino, for the material concerning experimental sensory deprivation which is included in Chapter 1.

Particular thanks are extended to Mrs. Rosanne Stein for her secretarial help during the preparation of this work, and to Miss Lee Barbieri for preparing the final manuscript and for helping in many other ways to get the book to press.

The work reported in this book was supported in part by research grant A-2504 and training grant 2A-5277 from the National Institute of Arthritis and Metabolic Diseases, National Institutes of Health. One of us (RGP) carried out these studies during a postdoctoral traineeship of this Institute.

The authors are indebted to the J. B. Lippincott Co. for permission to reprint Figures 8 and 10, which originally appeared in *Emotional Problems of Childhood,* edited by Samuel Liebman, 1958, Chapter 2 (Observations on the Psychological Development of Infants, Julius B. Richmond and Earle L. Lipton). The quotation at the beginning of Chapter 4 from *Of Mice and Men* by John Steinbeck is copyright 1938 by John Steinbeck and is reprinted by permission of The Viking Press, Inc.

R.G.P.

L.I.G.

Contents

List of Illustrations

GROWTH FAILURE IN MATERNAL DEPRIVATION

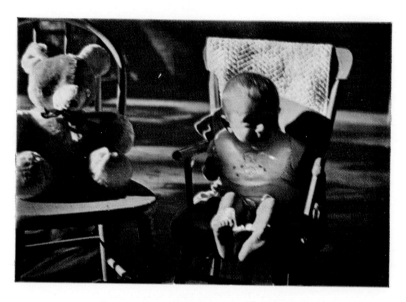

" . . . A Doll in a Teacup She Were."

This line from Kipling expresses the clinical picture seen in the little girl shown here. She was in the early hospital recovery phase of maternal deprivation with growth retardation. Because of her extremely small size for age, this infant seemed like an unusually well-coordinated doll. She also exhibited the "radar gaze" phenomenon of the post-maternal deprivation period, tracking every person in range of her bright eyes.

Chapter 1

Experimental Sensory Deprivation and Its Possible Relationship to the Syndrome of Maternal Deprivation

Shipwrecked individuals or those who for some reason fail to receive adequate environmental stimulation often describe loss of contact with their environment and loss of appetite. It has also been observed that psychologically deprived infants and children frequently show a decreased growth rate despite adequate physical care. The effect of sensory input on feeding and growth is an important aspect of observations on human sensory deprivation.

3

One of the earliest animal experiments on the effect of isolation upon body weight was done in 1931 by Vetulani (2). Using 130 closely inbred mice, he followed the growth of these animals from the sixth to the twenty-second week of life. Sixty-nine male mice and sixty-one female mice were divided into four groups each, with the sexes separate. The groupings were as follows:

Group	No. Mice/Cage
a	1
b	2–4
c	5–6
d	9–12

Among the males, Vetulani noted that those animals in groups of two to four per cage weighed the most, isolated animals weighed the least, and the other groups were intermediate in weight. Among the females, the isolated animals grew more rapidly than did the grouped animals. At the end of twenty-two weeks, the experimenter isolated certain animals from groups b, c and d and rearranged the group animals into groups of four. After ten weeks, he noted that among both males and females the isolated ones grew least while the mice grouped two to four per cage grew best. It was also observed that the isolated animals seemed irritable.

In 1932, an investigator specifically attempted to reduce visual stimulation (3). The eyelids of young dogs and cats were sewed together. Upon later examination, he observed in these animals a thinner occipital cortex with narrow convolutions and fewer Nissl granules. Twenty years later Brattgard reared rabbits ten weeks in darkness and found that the retinal ganglion cells showed an absence of pentose nucleoproteins (4).

In 1943, Wolf tried to determine at what age stimulus deprivation would exert the greatest effect on behavior (5). He divided seven litters of new-born albino rats into three groups as follows:

    I. Ears sealed with cotton and paraffin at ten days of age.

    II. Head encased in paraffin with openings for nose, mouth and ears at twelve to fifteen days old.

   III. No deprivation.

At the end of twenty-five days, which marks the end of the nursing period, all seals were removed and the animals isolated in individual cages for fourteen days. During this two week period, no attempt was made either to reduce stimulation or to disturb the animals in any way. Then the groups were tested in various stress situations, some of which required visual cues and others auditory cues. Those animals deprived of hearing won 62 per cent of the visual tests and 38 per cent of the auditory tests. If the eyes and ears of the rats were sealed after the animals were fifty and seventy-three days old, no differences were noted in the performance of these animals, regardless of which sense had been blocked. Only when the animals were deprived of light or sound during the weanling period was their behavior as adults affected and then only when the animal was stressed.

In 1947, Riesen observed feeding behavior in a male and female chimpanzee which were reared in darkness until they were sixteen months old (6). After this time, the animals were periodically brought into the light for observation. On the eleventh day after exposure to light, the female first seemed to recognize a feeding bottle by protruding her lips towards it. On the sixteenth day she first reached for the bottle. This was definitely retarded performance since she was sixteen months old and normal animals reach for a bottle before they are twelve months old. The experimenter added that the bottle was offered late enough after a mealtime so that the animal should have been hungry. In another experiment, Riesen and Nissen reared three chimpanzees in darkness from birth to seven, twenty and thirty-three months respectively and one from eight to twenty-four months (7). Although food intake was not reduced in these animals, all showed marked retardation in the ossification of their epiphyses. This finding is very important in respect to the retardation in osseous maturation seen in children with maternal deprivation (see Chap. 4).

The question of how stimulation influences feeding behavior was investigated in several experiments in the 1950's. Amsel and Maltzman trained twenty female albino rats, 120 to 150 days old, to drink water for ten minutes each day for fourteen days (8). In a three day experimental period, the animals were electroshocked before drinking, ten animals on one day and ten on the next. A shock before drinking increased water consumption. These authors concluded that an increase in total drive strength in these animals enhanced water consumption.

In 1955, MacDonald and Teghtsoonian divided forty male albino rats into four groups of ten rats each (9). From the twenty-second to the forty-second day, these animals were exposed to varying degrees of light with a sixty-watt bulb as follows:

Group   I: No light/day
Group   II: Two hours of light/day
Group III: Eight hours of light/day
Group IV: Sixteen hours of light/day

The death of one of the Group III animals eliminated that group. At the forty-second day, no significant inter-group differences were found in the body weights of these animals. On day forty-three, each animal was exposed to intense light stimulation for three minutes. The animals were weighed each day afterwards for two weeks. By the end of this time, the group that had previously received sixteen hours/day of light stimulation weighed more than did any of the other groups. These workers concluded that in the rat visual stimulation intensified the drive level, which in turn influenced responses such as eating, thereby affecting gain in weight. Another interpretation held that while the brief but intense light stimulus stressed all of the animals, those animals which had received the most light previously were least affected. No observations of the adrenals were made in this experiment. If excessive stimulation or stimulus deprivation, or both, may be considered as forms of stress, comparison of the adrenals of these animals might have been informative, for animals exposed to a variety of stresses are known to show adrenal hypertrophy.

Some investigators have attempted to show how sensory deprivation may influence growth. In one such project, hooded rats nursed in litters of three grew faster than did those in litters of fifteen to twenty (10). At the same ages the fast-growing rats were more active than were the slow-growing animals. Similar correlations between litter size and growth were noted by Kennedy in 1957, a point to be discussed in more detail in Chapter 3 (11). Kennedy also studied the effect of specific brain lesions on growth. In the first twenty-four hours following hypothalamic lesion, presumably in the ventro-medial nuclei, a group of weanling rats ate twice as much as did controls. This over-eating was transient.

However, as growth leveled off, most grew fat, and one-third showed retarded skeletal growth. These dwarfed animals became obese sooner than did the rest of the rats, in which growth in length was not retarded. A slower plateauing of food intake with age apparently accounted for the obesity. Lesions in the posterior-medial eminence and in the mammillary bodies which did not affect appetite did seem to interfere with growth.

In an experiment in 1960, nose-tail length, tibial length, and body weight of seventy-one male albino rats with hypothalamic lesions were compared with paired controls and thirty *ad libitum* fed animals (12). Most of the lesion-bearing animals ate as much or more than did control animals. In all animals with extensive lesions measurements of tibial length revealed impaired growth. No adrenal cortical insufficiency was demonstrated. Administration of thyroxine, testosterone, and pitressin failed to restore normal growth. The most severe depression of the usual growth rate, 59.7 per cent to 66.9 per cent of normal, was seen in animals with lesions of the anterior half of the median eminence. There was no evidence that the hypophyseal blood supply had been disrupted. This experiment supports the hypothesis that growth hormone secretion may in part be controlled by the hypothalamus.

It is of interest to note that differences in weight curves have been observed in rats subjected to gentling during early life (13-16).

Hebb noted that dogs reared in isolation had no obvious physical disability although their social responses seemed atypical (17). Thompson and Melzack have reviewed their own work, and that of others, concerned with the evaluation of the influence of early environmental deprivation on dogs (18). Although these studies did not deal with growth studies *per se,* the behavioral observations are of considerable interest because of certain similarities with the syndrome in human infants. Litters of Scottish terriers were weaned at age four weeks and divided into two groups. One group was raised normally as controls. The dogs of the other group were each confined in a separate cage. The cage was built so that the puppy could not see outside because of opaque walls. By constructing a "dining room" as a second compartment, the dog could be fed and his cage cleaned without the subject ever seeing his keepers. The experimental puppies were kept in this isolated environment until they were seven to ten months old. At this time the two groups of dogs were reunited in the laboratory and compared with respect to behavior.

The deprived dogs showed what was described as a puppylike exuberance that was disproportionately juvenile for their age. Investigation of this phenomenon by psychological testing indicated that the deprived dogs did indeed have behavioral immaturity as evidenced, in part, by abnormally increased curiosity about their environment. Prolonged testing of these dogs also showed that the effects of their early restriction were present for several years after they left their early cages.

These findings are reminiscent of behavior in human maternal deprivation. The "puppylike exuberance" of the recovery phase of the deprived dogs may be compared with the "doll in a teacup" phase of the human infant during the recovery phase after a period of maternal deprivation. Observers have noted the bright-eyed, over-curiosity of these abnormally small infants. Their behavior in the hospital ward has been described as a "radar gaze," since they tend to search out and follow, with their eyes, every moving person in the room.

Thompson and Melzack also tested their Scotties' intelligence with eighteen maze problems. They found that the deprived dogs' performance on these problems was considerably below that of the controls. They made about 50 per cent more errors. Again dogs who had been post-deprivation for several years still scored below their litter-mate controls, suggesting that the effects of early deprivation on intelligence as tested in this experiment were very prolonged, and possibly permanent. As will be pointed out in later chapters, abnormalities in the psychological testing of children with maternal deprivation may persist into the adolescent years, and perhaps even longer.

Since these and other experiments suggest that the hypothalamus is involved in the regulation of appetite and of growth, the question arises as to how such hypothalamic influence correlates with sensory deprivation. When the reticular activating system is affected through decreased sensory inputs, Kubzansky and Leiderman have postulated that cortical factors, now not under control of the reticular activating system, may play a more prominent role.

They suggest that this relative change in the balance between reticular activating system function and cortical activity is associated with some of the behavioral findings in sensory deprivation (19). Gellhorn has postulated that there are interconnections between the reticular formation and the hypothalamus (20). In sensory deprivation, alterations in sensory input affect hypothalamic activity via the reticular activating system, to which visual and auditory fibers give collaterals. Herein, he concludes, the sensory and the parasympathetic and sympathetic branches of the nervous system are interconnected.

In 1915, a survey made in Baltimore by Knox revealed that despite adequate physical care 90 per cent of infants in institutions died within one year of admission (21). Infants under six months old in these institutions had an indifferent appetite, failed to gain weight and in order to gain the same amount of weight as infants at home, were said to have needed much more food. This survey noted that growth in height was normal or only slightly decreased. In Bellefaire, a children's home in Ohio, the incidence of growth failure was high in those children who had been institutionalized because of neglect (22). Later Spitz described among institutionalized children a syndrome which he termed anaclitic depression. In one such institution, "Foundling Home," he observed that infants six to eleven months old failed to respond to stimuli, seemed depressed and lost appetite and weight (23). By the age of two, most could not eat alone. Two-year olds who had been in another home, "Nursery," had left at about age one year, were active and could eat with a spoon. In the latter home it was believed that the children received more individual attention. Developmental progress appeared to correlate not only with the length of stay but also with the attention received while the infants were in the foundling homes.

Engel *et al.* have more recently observed a girl born with congenital atresia of the esophagus (24). Fearing dislodgement of the gastric tube through which the infant was fed, the mother had tended not to cuddle the child. At fifteen months of age, the child showed the physical development of a five to eight month old child and refused to suck the sugar nipple which the mother had been instructed to give the infant during the tube feedings. Upon hospital admission, the child showed decreased gastric HCL and pepsin. Histamine failed to evoke an acid secretion. During a nine-month hospital admission in which she received more attention than previously, the child's weight rose from 4500 to 7500 g.

Effects of stimulus-deprivation upon adults have been studied in an experiment in which eighteen human volunteers were confined for one to three days in a dark, lightproof, soundproof room (25). *Ad libitum* feeding consisted of soup, water, sandwiches and fruit. Although all ate well, sometimes more than normal since eating helped overcome boredom, all but one lost weight. Except for one individual, the controls showed little change in weight. Among the experimentals, the average weight loss for the three periods were as follows:

Hours of Isolation	Weight Loss (lbs.)
24	2.7
48	1.7
72	2.5

One man in the 72-hour group lost 4.5 lbs. Afterwards, most subjects described a lack of interest in the food. By the end of the first day after being released from confinement nearly one-half the lost weight was regained. In another experiment in which human volunteers were placed in a similar soundproof room for varying amounts of time, the subjects also received an unlimited supply of food. While these persons enjoyed preparing meals, most described eating as a mechanical procedure. Food seemed flat and unenjoyable. To most of the subjects, all foods within one category, such as meat, tasted alike (25).

As the foregoing brief account indicates, there are relatively few experimental studies which bear directly on the problem of growth retardation as related either to sensory deprivation or to adverse maternal-infant interaction. The clinical studies to be reported in the succeeding chapters of this volume will be oriented to the problems of retarded physical growth and development which are encountered in situations where there is disturbance of the mother-infant relationship and/or other abnormalities in the milieu of the family—the syndrome now usually termed maternal deprivation.

For the sake of completeness the attention of the reader should be called to two recent reviews of maternal deprivation which provide extensive bibliographic resources. The review of Yarrow is limited to studies on human subjects (26). Casler's review includes both animal experimentation and observations on children (27). Both reviews deal principally with the behavioral aspects of maternal deprivation. Casler's sections on animal experimentation and neuroanatomical hypotheses are especially relevant. Important reports have also recently been published by the W.H.O. (28) and by the Child Welfare League of America (29).

References

1. Green, R. M.: *A Translation of Galen's Hygiene (De Sanitate Tuenda).* Springfield, Thomas, p. 24, 1951.

2. Vetulani, T.: Cited in W. C. Allee: *Handbook of Social Psychology.* Worcester, Clark University Press, p. 927, 1935.

3. Goodman, L.: Effect of total absence of function on the optic system of rabbit. *Am. J. Physiol., 100*:46, 1932.

4. Brattgard, S.: The importance of adequate stimulation for the chemical composition of retinal ganglion cells during early post-natal development. *Acta. Radiol. supp., 96* (1952); Cited in F. Beach and J. Jaynes: Effects of early experience upon the behavior of animals. *Psychol. Bull., 51*:239, 1952.

5. Wolf, A.: The dynamics of the selective inhibition of specific function in neurones. *Psychosomatic Med., 5*:27, 1943.

6. Riesen, A.: The development of visual perception in man and chimpanzee. *Science, 106*:107, 1947.

7. Riesen, A. and Nissen, H.: Retardation of onset of ossification in chimpanzees. *Anat. Rec., 105*:665, Dec. 1949.

8. Amsel, A. and Maltzman, I.: The effect upon generalized drive strength of emotionality as inferred from the level of consummatory response. *J. Exper. Psychol., 40*:563, 1950.

9. Brewer, N. R., Ed.: *Animal Care Panel* (Chicago: Animal Care Panel, Inc., 1955), p. 70.

10. Làt, J., Widdowson, E. M. and McCance, R. A.: Some effects of accelerating growth. III. Behavior and nervous activity. *Proc. Roy. Soc. London, B, 153*:347, 1960.

11. Kennedy, G. C.: The development with age of hypothalamic restraint upon the appetite of the rat. *J. Endocrinol., 16*:9, Nov. 1959.

12. Reichlin, S.: Growth and the hypothalamus. *Endocrinology, 67*: 760, Dec. 1960.

13. Ruegamer, W. R., Bernstein, L. and Benjamin, J. D.: Growth, food utilization, and thyroid activity in the albino rat as a function of extra handling. *Science, 120*:184, 1954.

14. Ruegamer, W. R. and Silverman, F. R.: Influence of gentling on physiology of the rat. *Proc. Soc. Exper. Biol. & Med., 92*:170, 1956.

15. Bovard, E. W. and Newton, D. G.: Systematic early handling and prolonged experience with the mother as developmental variables in the male albino rat. *Animal Care Panel Proc., 6*:67, 1955.

16. Newton, G., Bly, C. G. and McCrary, C.: Cage dimension, handling and weight gain. *Psychol. Reports, 6*:355-357, 1960.

17. Hebb, O.: Motivating effects of exteroceptive stimulation. *Am. Psychol., 13*:110, 1958.

18. Thompson, W. R. and Melzack, R.: Early environment: How do environmental influences at the beginning of life shape the behavior of an animal? *Scientific American, 194*:38, Jan. 1956.

19. Kubzansky, P. E. and Leiderman, P. H.: Chap. 15 in Solomon, P. *et al.*, Ed.: *Sensory Deprivation.* Cambridge, Harvard University Press, 1961.

20. Gellhorn, E.: Quoted by Kubzansky and Leiderman, *Idem.* (19).

21. Knox, J., quoted by Chapin, H. D.: A plea for accurate statistics in infants' institutions, *Tr. Am. Ped. Soc., 27*:180, 1915; Cited in Bakwin, H.: Emotional deprivation in infants. *J. Pediat., 35*:512, Oct. 1949.

22. Fried, R. and Mayer, M.: Socio-economic factors accounting for growth failure in children living in institutions. *J. Pediat., 33*: 445, 1948.

23. Spitz, R. A.: Anaclitic depression, in *The Psychoanalytic Study of the Child, II.* New York, International Univ. Press, p. 113, 1946.

24. Engel, G. L. and Reichsman, F.: Spontaneous and experimentally induced depressions in an infant with a gastric fistula—a contribution to the problem of depression. *J. Am. Psychoanalyt. A., 4*:428, (July) 1956.

25. Vernon, J. A., McGill, T. E., Gulick, W. L. and Candland, D. R., Chap. 4 in Solomon, P. et al.: *Ibid.* (19).
26. Yarrow, L. J.: Maternal deprivation: Toward an empirical and conceptual reevaluation. *Psychological Bull., 58*:459-490, Nov. 1961.
27. Casler, L.: Maternal deprivation: A critical review of the literature. Monographs Soc. for Research in Child Development, Vol. 26, No. 2, Serial No. 80, 50 pp., 1961.
28. Ainsworth, M. D., Andry, R. G., Harlow, R. G., Lebovici, S., Mead, M., Prugh, D. G. and Wootton, B. (contributors): *Deprivation of Maternal Care: A Reassessment of its Effects.* Geneva, World Health Organization, Public Health Papers No. 14, 165 pp., 1962.
29. Yarrow, L. J., Ainsworth, M. D. and Glaser, K. (contributors): *Maternal Deprivation.* (Papers read at the Eastern Regional Conference, Child Welfare League of America, New York, N. Y., April 1961.) New York, N. Y., Child Welfare League of America, Inc., 72 pp., 1962.

Chapter 2

His second folly was that he wanted to find out what kind of speech and what manner of speech children would have when they grew up, if they spoke to no one beforehand. So he bade foster mothers and nurses to suckle the children, to bathe and to wash them, but in no way to prattle with them or to speak to them, for he wanted to learn whether they would speak the Hebrew language, which was the oldest, or Greek, or Latin, or Arabic, or perhaps the language of their parents, of whom they had been born. But he laboured in vain, because the children all died. For they could not live without the petting and the joyful faces and loving words of their foster mothers.

SALIMBENE—13th century (1, 2)

The Clinical Picture of Maternal Deprivation with Associated Failure to Thrive

This account by a medieval historian describes an experiment performed by the Emperor Frederick II. Designed to investigate the origins of speech, its unexpected conclusion served to illustrate the importance of a very fundamental determinant of infant growth and development. The status of these less easily definable aspects of infant and child care as "biologically necessary" has been somewhat eclipsed in recent years by the more quantitative contributions of the basic sciences. The renewed interest in the importance of social and emotional factors in human infant growth is in no way antagonistic, but is, in fact, complementary to molecular biology. These two areas of interest should be considered points in a continuum, whose relationships will become clearer as more knowledge is gained about the role of the central nervous system in the regulation of metabolic processes.

Influenced by the economic abundance of our society, and by current orientations in medicine, one's intuitive approach toward the etiology of severe delay in growth and development would be in the direction of specific hormonal or metabolic disorders, of genetic determination, or of disturbances in the intrauterine or perinatal environment. It is of considerable interest, then, that, in the authors' experience, the syndrome of growth retardation, delayed osseous maturation, and retardation of motor and intellectual development has often been associated with gross disturbance of the child's social and emotional environment. This type of environmental disorder has generally been referred to as "deprivation." The degree of reversibility of these findings, after improvement in the environment, has been variable. There has been a tendency for these children to show very striking initial improvement, in physical growth as well as in emotional and intellectual development, but to remain below the age norms during the periods of followup, which have varied in length from six months to seven years in the cases presented here.

Deprivation is a rather vague and inclusive term, and it will be one of the purposes of this paper to give it closer definition. It may encompass deficiency in calories, protein or other essential nutrients, exposure to extremes of physical environment, trauma, social isolation, and disruption of the usual physical and emotional bonds between the infant and his mother. Many or all of these factors seem to be operative in the cases presented in this volume, but it is the last which seems to be the most evident and commonly present one, and to be the focal point about which the others stand in secondary position. As used in this volume, then, the term "deprivation" implies a state in which the disturbance of the mother-infant relationship is primary, and the various physical alterations in the environment are secondary, and is meant to be generally synonymous with the terms "maternal deprivation," "hospitalism," and "anaclitic depression." Although the characteristic pattern of behavior and the delay in intellectual and motor development are integral features of the syndrome, and will be discussed, the authors have been especially interested in extreme retardation of growth and of epiphyseal maturation as associated findings in this disorder, and in the ways in which social and emotional factors may be involved etiologically. The cases presented, therefore, are those of infants and children whose presenting problem was that of growth failure. They have been selected as being typical of the maternal deprivation syndrome, and are not meant to represent a total compilation of the authors' experience with this problem. Others have not been included because adequate environmental histories have been unavailable, and other children with significant organic disease have not been included, even though deprivation has appeared to be an important additive factor in the etiology of the growth failure.

The deprivation in the cases to follow has consisted of neglect, rejection, and isolation from normal social contacts, although physical abuse and intentional malnutrition have been occasionally associated. It is more closely related to social and emotional disorders within the family than to economic status, and, in fact, has been described in families of relatively high socio-economic position. Six such children, each of whom was first brought to medical attention because of delayed growth or "failure to thrive," are described here. In each case, the syndrome developed while the child was living in the home with its mother, although the clinical features seem to be almost identical with those previously described in institutionalized infants, and called "hospitalism" and "anaclitic depression." The present study is especially oriented toward the effects of this condition on physical growth.

Methods

Height-age was determined as the age for which the actual height represented the 50th percentile value, using charts constructed by H. C. Stuart and associates at the Harvard School of Public Health. Weight-age was similarly derived. Bone age was determined from x-rays of the wrist and fingers, using the atlas of Greulich and Pyle, 1959.

Review of Clinical Studies

Clinical observations on the six children will first be presented in summary form, as a prelude to the discussion which will follow in Chapter 3. The cases will be described in greater detail in Chapter 4.

Case 1 (D.S.) exemplifies some of the findings in the group of infants. This girl was first seen at age fifteen months because of growth failure. During the first month of life she had some feeding difficulties but thereafter she was said to have had an excellent, almost ravenous appetite. Vitamin supplementation appeared to be adequate by history. Solid foods were begun early and taken well. Despite this the child failed to gain weight and exhibited lethargic behavior, sleeping sixteen to eighteen hours daily. In the two months prior to first hospital admission she lost two pounds.

The mother's childhood had been marked by rejection and extreme domestic instability. She was said to have a "violent hatred" of her child (the patient). The father was described as an "inadequate person" who worked only sporadically and was an alcoholic. He disclaimed the patient as his own child. She was kept isolated in a dark room.

The infant appeared much less mature than her actual age, was malnourished and extremely retarded in growth (see Fig. 1). She was very lethargic and withdrawn, and ignored the examiner. There was no evidence of physical trauma. Physical examination revealed no abnormalities of the major organ systems, or neurological changes. The extremities were thin and poorly muscled.

Case 4 (R.A.) is that of an older child, six and one-half year old boy, who was also first seen because of extreme growth retardation. Despite some neonatal feeding difficulties, early growth was felt to be satisfactory, and it was not until the age of twenty months that his mother felt that growth "stopped." X-rays, taken at another hospital when the boy was four, showed a bone age of eighteen months. Films of the wrist at five and one-half years of age showed ossification at the two and one-half year level. He was said to be very sensitive and shy, unable to integrate socially with his peers, and had enuresis and encopresis. The diet, as described, was nutritionally adequate.

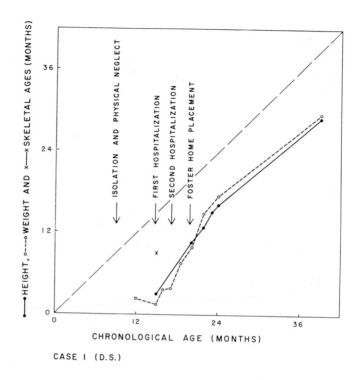

CASE I (D.S.)

Fig. 1. Growth chart of patient D.S. (Case 1). Chronological age in months is plotted on the abscissa. Height-age, weight-age and skeletal age in months are shown on the ordinate. The transverse dotted line indicates the 50th percentile developmentally. The initial measurements on this girl are far below this line, denoting gross retardation in physical development. Observe the very rapid improvement in height and weight for the first several months after the first hospitalization. The slope of the curve changed at about twenty-four months of age to a slower velocity of growth. Since the osseous development was relatively less retarded than linear growth, the growth chart of this girl shows a Wilkins type II pattern.

The mother was well, 5′4″, and a brother, three, and a sister, two, were of normal size. The father, 5′11″, had worked only occasionally, and living conditions for the family had always been inadequate and temporary. There were frequent violent disagreements between the parents, and the father was away from the home

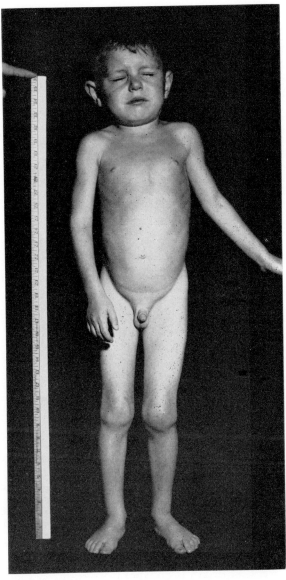

Fig. 2. Patient R.A. (Case 4) when first seen at age six and one-half years. His height was that of a three and one-half year old, and his osseous development was even less than that. Encopresis and enuresis were prominent problems. He was being cared for by transient baby-sitters, since his mother had to work to support the family.

much of the time. The mother had been forced to support the family, occasionally holding two jobs at once, and thus was away from home throughout much of the day. During this time the patient was cared for by various relatives and "friends." The quality of care was frequently rather poor, and "black and blue spots" were noted on more than one occasion.

Examination revealed an extremely small boy of six and one-half, who did not appear malnourished and was normally proportioned for his age (see Fig. 2). His height was 99.8 cm. (height age was three and one-half years) and his weight 12.9 Kg. Skin texture and temperature were normal, and the hair was fine. Dentition was normal for age. There were no other physical abnormalities.

Laboratory data were all within normal limits. The I^{131} uptake was sixteen per cent in twenty-four hours, and the serum protein-bound iodine was 7.5 micrograms per cent. Roentgenographic findings were normal, except for a bone age of two and one-half years.

As shown in Table I, five of these children were first seen between the ages of thirteen and thirty-six months, the other one (Case 4) at six and one-half years. Height ages were from 20 per cent to 65 per cent of the actual ages, with a mean of 42 per cent. All of the five younger children were extremely underweight and appeared malnourished. Bone-ages were from 20 per cent to 67 per cent of the actual ages, also with a mean of 42 per cent. The bone-age height age ratios varied from 0.56 to 2.0 with a mean of 1.1. Dentition was normal for the actual ages. The five younger children were all retarded in development. None was walking alone. Only the thirty-six month old child was talking, and he only with a few unintelligible single words. All were lethargic, apathetic and withdrawn in their behavior. Exaggerated rhythmic body movements were frequently seen. The six and one-half year old boy was extremely shy, unable to form good relationships with his peers, and had enuresis and encopresis.

There were no physical or laboratory findings suggesting the presence of any specific endocrine or metabolic disorder, or of significant pathology in any major organ system which could be responsible for the growth failure. There was mild nutritional anemia in Cases 2, 3 and 5.

TABLE I

Case	Chronological Age	Length Cm.	Height Age Mos.	Weight Kg.	Bone Age Mos.
1	15.0 mos.	58.0	3	4.4	6
2	36.0 mos.	72.5	12	7.0	15
3	13.5 mos.	69.0	9	4.5	6
4	6.5 yrs.	99.8	42	12.9	30
5	22.0 mos.	67.5	8.0	6.0	4.5
6	18.0 mos.	70.0	9.0	7.7	12

Roentgenographic findings, in addition to the retarded bone-ages, were those of dense transverse lines of growth arrest at the ends of the long bones, and of osteoporosis in one case (infant 3).

There was no history of growth retardation among parents or other relatives, with the exception of siblings of infants 4 and 6. All of these children were products of grossly disturbed family environments, characterized by emotional disorders in the parents, separation of the parents, alcoholism, and other socially undesirable behavior. Although economic conditions were poor, sufficient food for adequate nutrition of the children was available through welfare agencies. As far as could be determined, an adequate diet was provided to all of these children with the exception of infants 5 and 6.

The oldest patient (Case 4), who has been followed for a period of seven years, had a remarkable acceleration of growth between the ages of eight and ten, which correspond in time with a great improvement in the home situation (see Fig. 3). Between ages ten and fourteen there was even greater growth velocity with full adolescent development (see Fig. 4). Among the five younger children, there was a favorable response to hospitalization, with rapid weight gain, and with much improvement in mood, social responsiveness, and in language and motor abilities. These children were then placed in supervised foster homes. This was done only after

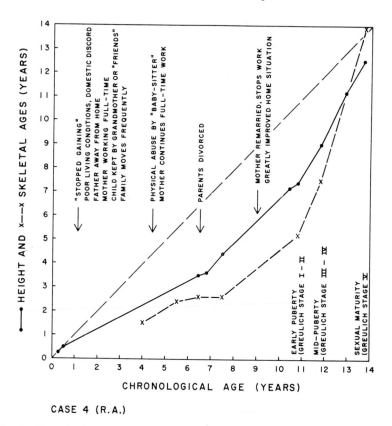

CASE 4 (R.A.)

Fig. 3. Growth chart of patient R.A. (Case 4). Note that his retardation of osseous development was much greater than retardation of linear growth (Wilkins type I). The vicissitudes of his early life are described on the chart. His development of puberty with a markedly retarded bone age is here documented. The writers are not aware of any previous description of such a phenomenon.

repeated attempts by the domestic courts and social agencies to attain a satisfactory environment of the child in his own home, and it was hoped that this placement would be temporary in most cases. After this period of initial rapid improvement, however, the rate of increase in linear growth, weight gain, and skeletal maturation has been variable, with most of these parameters remaining below the fiftieth percentile for age during the periods of study.

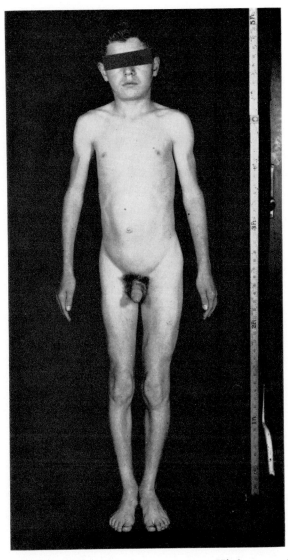

Fig. 4. Patient R.A. (Case 4) at age fourteen years. His bone age has attained a developmental pattern normal for his age. He still had emotional problems, as exemplified by school failure, enuresis, encopresis and inadequate social adaptation.

In some cases, follow-up periods have been less than one year, which places limitations on the conclusions which can be drawn from the data. It does appear, however, that these children are limited in their ability to regain a normal growth pattern, even after correction of the environmental deficiencies. It is difficult to determine whether this is due to inheritance, or to a permanent reduction in growth potential caused by the unfavorable environmental circumstances of earlier childhood and infancy. Much the same can be said for the improvement in mood, social behavior, and intellectual function. The response to environmental change was initially quite favorable. The four younger children did not attain developmental and behavioral norms for age during the periods of study, however, and the two older children, who have been followed into late childhood, show evidence of some persistent damage to personality structure and intellect.

[References at end of Chap. V]

Chapter 3

> *All this vigilance and care could not make little Paul a thriving boy. Naturally delicate, perhaps, he pined and wasted after the dismissal of his nurse, and for a long time seemed but to wait his opportunity of gliding through their hands, and seeking his lost mother. This dangerous ground in his steeplechase towards manhood passed, he still found it very rough riding, and was grievously beset by all the obstacles in his course.*
>
> CHARLES DICKENS,
> *Dombey and Son,* Chap. 8, 1848

Observations and Discussion Concerning Maternal Deprivation

Social Background

It is immediately apparent that all of these children were products of grossly disordered family situations. In each of these families, one or both of the parents showed evidence of severe emotional disturbance and inability to cope with the usual responsibilities of parenthood. At least two of the mothers (and this would undoubtedly be true of others if adequate histories were available) were themselves products of such experiences in early childhood. This serves well to illustrate the importance of an individual's own experiences with his parents in determining his later effectiveness in the parental role (3). Of the fathers, only three

25

were still living with the families when these studies were begun. Of these three, however, none was able to maintain steady employment, one was a chronic alcoholic, and in all cases the relationship between the parents was violently disharmonious. In one case (Case 3) the mother was mentally deficient and the father an habitual criminal.

Economic conditions were poor in all families, but all were under the surveillance of welfare agencies, and sufficient food to maintain adequate nutrition could have been obtained at all times.

Previous Medical History

The birth weights of these children ranged from 4 lb. 4 oz. (1.9 kg.) to 7 lb. 3 oz. (3.3 kg.). Two of them were premature by gestational age (Cases 4 and 5), but neither required prolonged nursery care. In Case 1 there had been rupture of the membranes during the second trimester of pregnancy, and pre-eclampsia.

Although actual measurements are lacking in most cases, there was no history of growth retardation among the parents or other near relatives. There was growth delay among siblings in Cases 4 and 6.

Early feeding difficulties included diarrhea, rumination, persistent vomiting, refusal of bottle and refusal to take solid foods. Dietary histories, which must be viewed with some skepticism, indicated that adequate diets were provided in Cases 1, 2, 3, and 4. Milk was the only food provided in Case 5, and in Case 6 there is good evidence for general undernutrition. Vitamin supplements were given to all except Cases 5 and 6. There was no correlation between the adequacy of the diet as determined by history and the apparent nutritional status, the growth pattern, or the behavior of the child.

Physical care was passively neglectful in all instances, with the probable exception of Case 4. Physical trauma occurred in Case 1, and cold injury to the extremities was found in Cases 3 and 6.

There were no previous severe illnesses, other than an episode of "bowel obstruction" (medically treated) in Case 6. Frequent upper respiratory infections and bouts of diarrhea were reported in Cases 1 and 2. Severe constipation was present in Cases 1 and 6.

Psychomotor development was generally retarded in Cases 2, 5, and 6, moderately so in Case 4. It is interesting, however, that in Cases 1 and 3, there is good documentation of normal development during the first four to five months of life, with later deterioration.

Although not easy to assess, there were considerable differences in the maternal attitudes toward the affected children. In Cases 1 and 6 there was frank hostility, often expressed overtly, and in Case 5, hostility and "disgust." Indifference and annoyance characterized the feelings of the mother in Case 2, and this mother also felt that the child "hated" her. In Case 4, the mother expressed concern for the child but was caught up in circumstances which prevented the normal expression of her maternal feelings. In Case 3, the mother was mentally defective.

Initial Physical Findings

The children, who varied in age from thirteen months to six and one-half years, were all severely retarded in growth (this being the reason for which medical attention was first sought). Height-ages were from 20 per cent to 65 per cent of the chronological ages, with a mean figure of 42 per cent. All of these children appeared malnourished, with decreased subcutaneous fat, and diminished muscle mass and tone. "Weight-ages" were significantly less than height-ages in all cases initially. Non-specific skin lesions (excoriated papular eruptions and pustular diaper rashes) were present in all cases, and two (Cases 3 and 6) had red and edematous extremities. These were probably related to cold injury. Body proportions were normal for the chronological ages, and there were no gross skeletal abnormalities. Dentition was normal for chronological ages in all instances. There were no pulmonary or cardiac abnormalities, and, although the liver was palpable in three children, none was considered to be abnormal. Except for the developmental retardation and behavioral changes described, there were no abnormal neurological findings.

Initial Emotional and Developmental Status

The five younger patients presented a strikingly similar pattern of emotional behavior. All were lethargic, apathetic and withdrawn. They did not smile, and avoided, with varying amounts of apparent anxiety, contact with other people. The most extreme example was seen in the "autistic" behavior of Case 6, with his absolute refusal to show recognition of people and objects in his immediate environment. His only response to such stimuli was to begin vigorous rhythmic, rocking movements. Rhythmic head shaking, nodding and banging were also prominent in Case 5. One of the infants (Case 3) held her hands cupped tightly over mouth and nose and vigorously resisted any attempts to remove them from this position.

The six and one-half year old boy (Case 4) was extremely shy, unable to get along socially with his age-mates, and had enuresis and encopresis.

Among the five younger children, there was extreme developmental retardation and a general depression of motor activity. None of these children was walking. Only the thirty-six month old boy was talking, and he with but a few unintelligible single words. The one older boy had begun to walk at nineteen months. Two of the infants (Cases 1 and 3) had exhibited more normal development and social behavior in the first few months of life, but had later regressed.

Laboratory Data

There was a moderate anemia in Cases 2, 3, and 5 (hemoglobins 8.7, 9.0 and 9.3 gm. per cent), which was believed to be due to lack of dietary iron, and which responded to iron therapy and to the inclusion of iron-containing foods in the diet. The finding of a serum iron of 61 micrograms per cent, and an iron binding capacity of only 137 micrograms per cent in Case 2 is difficult to explain, but this boy's mild anemia did respond to dietary measures. Serum proteins were normal in Cases 2 and 6, but low (4.8 gm. per cent) in Case 3. Blood nonprotein nitrogen and blood urea nitrogen values were normal, except for a borderline blood urea nitrogen of 21.5 mgm. per cent in Case 6. There was no other evidence of renal disease in this patient. Blood glucose values were normal where done (Cases 1, 4, and 6). Serum levels of calcium, phosphorus, and alkaline phosphatase activity were normal in Cases 2, 4, 5, and 6.

Stools were not grossly characteristic of steatorrhea or other malabsorption states and did not show excess fat or protein microscopically. In one case (Case 2), however, only 4.2 per cent of a nine gm. dose of d-xylose was excreted in the urine during the prescribed four hour period. Sweat electrolytes were normal in Cases 2 and 5. Serum protein-bound iodine determinations were normal in Cases 2, 4, 5, and 6.

Roentgenographic Findings

Bone-ages were estimated from bilateral hand and wrist films according to the standards of Greulich and Pyle (4), and varied from 20 per cent to 67 per cent of the chronological ages, with a mean figure of 42 per cent. Other centers were examined in three instances and were generally found to be at the same level of maturation as the hand centers. Anomalies of ossification, as described by Snodgrasse, *et al.* (5) and by Dreizen, *et al.* (6), were not noted in these children. Transverse lines at the ends of the long bones (particularly the distal ends of the radii) were very prominent in three children (Cases 1, 2, and 3) and present in two others (Cases 4 and 5). Osteoporosis was noted in Case 3. Chest, skull, gastrointestinal and urinary tract studies were normal.

Effects of Environmental Change

Among the five younger subjects there was noticeable improvement in mood, social responsiveness, and activity within the first few days of their hospitalization. This was delayed in Case 3, occurring only after the institution of very intensive personal care by one of the ward nurses, and in Case 6 the changes were less pronounced (this child had the most severe initial personality and behavior changes of this group).

In all instances there was also an acceleration of growth during this period. The increment in weight was greater than that in height or bone age.

In Cases 2, 5 and 6 followup periods have been short (six to eight months), after the transfer from hospital to foster homes. The acceleration of growth and of the attainment of social, language, and motor capabilities has continued during this time. Except for weight in Case 2, however, all of these developmental indices still stand short of age norms.

In those children (Cases 1, 3, and 4) where followups have been longer (2½ to 7 years), the outcome is still unclear. In Case 1, there was a rapid acceleration in weight gain and linear growth which lasted for about ten months. At this point, however, she seemed to "level off" in a channel well below the 50th percentile. There is little information about later emotional and intellectual development, except that she was felt by an observer to lack depth and spontaneity of affect at the age of five years.

In Case 3, the early growth acceleration involved weight gain only. There was little early acceleration in linear growth or in the rate of osseous maturation. This child, seven years later, remains well below the 50th percentile in weight, somewhat less so in height, but has by now regained normal bone age. Although superficially a happy girl, projective tests reveal persistent abnormalities in personality structure. Her dull normal I.Q. and poor school performance must be evaluated in terms of her genetic endowment (mentally defective mother) as well as her environmental history.

Case 4, first seen at the age of six and one-half years, had a remarkable acceleration of linear growth and skeletal maturation which began in his eighth year. This coincided in time with an appreciable improvement in the family's economic and emotional situation. This growth acceleration, however, extends into the preadolescent period, and this makes it more difficult to form definite opinions about the etiologic relationships. A remarkable dissociation between the bone age and the appearance of secondary sexual characteristics was seen. There was definite pubertal testicular enlargement when the bone age was five and one-half years, and secondary sex changes were well advanced when the bone age was seven and one-half years. In late puberty there was an acceleration of bone maturation, however, so that by fourteen years of age, the bone age was equal to the chronological age. Height remained below the 50th percentile at this time. Although he became more outgoing in his interpersonal relationships during his late childhood and early adolescence, the enuresis and encopresis continued, and educational progress was poor. His I.Q. (Otis) was 73, and a more recent California Mental Maturity test score 74.

Discussion

The Behavioral and Physiologic Effects of Infant Deprivation   In recent years there has been increasing interest in the effects of deprivation, and of infantile experience in general, on the development of the child, especially with regard to personality formation and intellectual function. The emotional and intellectual growth of the infant and child is no longer considered to be an entirely intrinsic phenomenon, which unfolds in a predetermined and unalterable fashion. Thus, while Gesell and Ilg speak of the "inborn sequence" and "inevitability" of growth mechanisms in the child, they also emphasize the contributions of social stimulation and "acculturation" to personality development, and say that "a personality cannot flourish except through interpersonal relationships" (7). Although couched in a different terminology, there is much similarity in the concept of the "undifferentiated psyche," whose optimum growth depends upon "a continuous relationship with a nurturient figure during the critical period of ego and superego development . . ." (8).

The participation of psychoanalytic theory in this concept of child development is further exemplified by the statement of Brody (9) that "direct observation of the ways that ego functions emerge in the infant indicates that they depend not only upon natural inborn structures which gradually mature in an orderly sequence, but that they also depend, from birth, upon primary identification with the behavior of persons in the environment, or upon reactions toward that behavior." In experimental psychology, too, there has been new interest in the role of perceptual activity on the development of learning ability and on personality formation. Animal experiments have shown the vital function of sensory experience in early life as a necessary foundation for learning capacity at maturity, and, in canines and primates, for normal "personality" structure (10).

Although there have been occasional studies of isolated and feral children (1, 11) and attempts to rear infants in an atmosphere devoid of social stimulation (12), most of the early observations of the effects of deprivation were those made of the behavior of children who had been institutionalized from birth or very early infancy. The emotional and intellectual effects of this sort of deprivation are well documented, and tend to fit a characteristic pattern. In 1941, Gesell and Amatruda (13) described the classic institutional syndrome, in which the infant lay on his back, exhibiting exaggerated forms of hand play, head nodding and head rolling, and other forms of stereotyped behavior, and refused to show recognition of surrounding objects or persons. This form of behavior was attributed to the paucity of sensory impacts in this "institutional silence." "Environmental impoverishment leads to behavioral impoverishment"—the institutional syndrome is then to be the result of a form of sensory deprivation. It is interesting in this regard that sectioning of the lemnisci in the midbrain of the cat, which deprives the cortex of afferent sensory connections, leads to "autistic" behavior on the part of the animal, which is in many ways similar to the behavior of the severely deprived infant (14).

It is now generally accepted that deprivation in infancy and early childhood may produce irrevocable damage to personality structure. Lowrey (15), in 1940, described aggressive, asocial, negativistic behavior, frequently accompanied by enuresis and speech defects, in children who had had the "isolation experience" of institutionalization during the first three years of their lives. Bowlby's (8) studies indicate that the effects of early deprivation may assume the form of the "psychopathic personality," with limited capacity for effective relationships, superficiality of emotional responses, and asocial behavior. He feels that these characteristics are most likely to appear in children whose deprivational experience in infancy has been severe enough to produce "apathetic withdrawal" with rhythmic rocking and head banging behavior, or in those deprived infants who show a cheerful, but undiscriminating and shallow attachment to any adult. Projective testing, by Goldfarb (16, 17) of children who had been institutionalized for the first three years of life, showed poor abstract thinking, poor control of emotional responses, and lack of drive toward intellectual achievement and social conformity. He also found that these children had "aggressive, distractible, uncontrolled behavior," and lacked the normal patterns of anxiety and self-inhibition. There was poor capacity for forming human identifications and relationships. This author also pointed out that these traits were not appreciably corrected by the normal family and social environment which the children had in later childhood.

In regard to this, it should be remembered that these children had been reared from birth to the age of three years in an environment which, although of highest hygienic standards, was quite sterile of interpersonal contact. Richmond and Hersher (18) have followed one of the patients in this series (Case 3) with periodic psychometric and personality testing, and have found that, despite excellent care and attention in her foster home situation, there is still evidence of disturbed intellectual and personality development. These findings imply that there are critical periods in the growth of personality, during which certain types of external stimulation are necessary for optimum development, and that, without these stimuli, permanent defects may result. There has been some recent experimental work which supports this. Freedman and co-workers (19) have shown that there are such critical periods in the social development of dogs. Their experiments showed that spaniels reared in the absence of human contact had an intense flight response when confronted with human beings. This response could be eliminated only if the pups were allowed to have contact with human beings between the ages of two and one-half and thirteen weeks, and it was shown that such contact was particularly effective at the age of seven weeks.

Intelligence, too, has been shown to be affected by deprivation in infancy, and these effects can be manifest as early as the third month of life. A rapid decline in the "developmental quotient," often to levels of severe retardation, was found to occur during the first two years of life in institutionalized infants by Spitz (20, 21). Ripin (22), in 1933, compared the development of infants in an institution with that of controls in homes of low economic status. After the age of six months, there was a steadily increasing difference in favor of the group reared in homes. Goldfarb (16, 17) studied a group of three year old children, half of whom had been in institutions since birth and half in foster homes from the age of four months. The intelligence quotients of the first group averaged 68, and of the latter group, 96.

There is less uniformity, however, among the studies which have been made concerning the reversibility of this retardation. Planned investigations and clinical observations alike have shown remarkable resurgence of developmental skills when deprived infants have been placed in more favorable environments. Clarke and Clarke (11) have shown considerable recovery by adolescent and young adult defectives, who had been severely deprived throughout childhood, when they were placed in a more favorable and stimulating environment. The greatest amount of recovery (relative to initial I.Q. scores) occurred in those who had had the most adverse situational backgrounds. Goldfarb (23, 17), on the other hand, found that, at the ages of ten to fourteen, there was still a difference in I.Q. of 23 points between family reared controls and children who had been institutionalized during the first three years of life. It will be remembered that, at three years of age, there had been an I.Q. difference of 28 points between similar groups of children.

These discrepancies are difficult to evaluate, primarily because of the difficulty in quantitating the amount of cultural stimulation which these children received, during the periods of deprivation and during "recovery." In summary, it can be said that intelligence is profoundly affected by early deprivation, that much recovery is possible with restoration of appropriate environmental stimulation, but that there may be critical periods of cerebral development in early childhood, during which the absence of cultural stimulation may cause permanent deficits. Also of certain importance are the amount and nature of the stimulation provided during the period of recovery.

Despite the predominant interest in emotional and intellectual development of the deprived infant, several early studies gave equal emphasis to the severe concomitant "physiologic" changes. Bakwin (24, 25) described the institutionalized infant with his listlessness, apathy and depression, failure to gain weight despite adequate nutritional intake, frequent stools, persistent respiratory infections, and unexplained fevers, all of which responded quickly to the return of the infant to his home and mother. He assigned these changes to the "emotionally arid atmosphere" of the hospitals, and suggested that deprivation was a primary cause of the high infant mortality in institutions, which existed up until the third decade of this century. Ribble (35), in 1944, described infantile reactions to inadequate "mothering," which were characterized by a "depressive and regressive quiescence," stupor, decreased muscle tone, regurgitation, diarrhea and malabsorption, even progressing to marasmus, respiratory irregularity, and a shock-like state. This syndrome was frequently seen as a result of prolonged hospitalization or institutionalization, and regularly responded well to the close attention of the mother or mother substitute. The author stated that the lack of mothering was "in no sense a casual matter of sentiment, but an actual privation which may result in biological, as well as psychological, damage to the infant."

Spitz and Wolff (21), in 1946, published their well known descriptions of this reaction to maternal deprivation, calling it "anaclitic depression." They described nursery infants, separated from their mothers in the latter half of the first year (which they considered to be the most vulnerable age), who responded with a pattern of behavior including apprehension, dejection, withdrawal and rejection of environment, slow movement and stupor and with anorexia and weight loss, insomnia, eczema, and frequent respiratory infections. When the infants were returned to their mothers these symptoms disappeared, but if separation was continued for more than three or four months, the infants entered a more malignant phase, characterized by further withdrawal, persistent autoerotic activities, "frozen rigidity," "stuporous catatonia," and cachexia. Of ninety-one foundling home infants studied, who were never returned to their mothers, thirty-four died "in spite of good food and meticulous medical care," and of twenty-one remaining in the institution, all had extreme retardation of growth and development. Of these infants, who ranged in age from two and one-half to four and one-fourth years, only five walked, and only one had a vocabulary of as much as twelve words. All were below the two-year norms for height and weight.

At this point, it might be well to mention some evidence that the rate of growth and physical maturation itself may have some effect on the development of intellectual and motor skills. Tanner

(27) has cited evidence that children who are physically advanced have higher intelligence quotients than age-mates who are smaller and less mature. More recently, Lat, Widdowson, and McCance (28) have shown definite behavioral differences between rats with accelerated growth and those who grew more slowly (though at normal rates). The more rapidly growing animals were consistently more active and inquisitive throughout the growing period. This effect has been observed whether the increased growth rate was nutritionally produced or genetically determined. These data are mentioned only to point out the possibility that developmental retardation in deprived infants may be related in some degree to the general delay in somatic growth, as well as to the lack of appropriate environmental stimulation.

Social Factors Related to Infant Deprivation   The earlier studies of deprivation which we have been reviewing are all concerned with infants and children who did poorly in institutions and who improved on returning to their homes. On the other hand, the cases which we have presented here are those of children who were not thriving in their homes, and with their natural mothers, but who improved with hospitalization and eventual placement in foster homes. This change in emphasis results from the fact that, in our socioeconomic setting, the "institutional syndrome" and "hospitalism" have been considerably replaced by deprivational situations occurring within the home. This, in turn, is a reflection of the advent of more enlightened methods of infant care in hospitals, and of the replacement of "foundling homes" by foster home care for homeless children (25).

It becomes apparent, then, that deprivation and separation from mother are not absolutely interchangeable terms. Engel and Reichsman's (29) important investigations were of an infant with esophageal atresia and a gastrostomy whose extreme depression, motor retardation, and failure to thrive were related to her mother's inability to establish the usual physical and emotional contacts with her child. This child, then, who did poorly while at home with her family, had an excellent response to hospitalization, in physical growth as well as emotional status. Coleman and Provence (30) have shown that developmental retardation due to deprivation can occur within the family setting, and even in families of relatively high socioeconomic status. Their patients had significant retardation of growth as well as of psychomotor development. This was related to disturbed, rejecting behavior on the part of the mothers, who, despite their physical presence, were unable to provide the sort of emotional environment necessary for normal infant development. There was a good response, both to change in environment for the child, and to change in maternal attitudes through psychotherapy.

Elmer (31) has described five infants, hospitalized because of "failure to thrive," and presenting the typical features of "hospitalism" although they had been living with their mothers. In each instance, a disturbance of the social environment was the major etiologic factor, and in some cases these disturbances were correctable by psychotherapy of the parents and other such methods, thereby circumventing the necessity of removing the child from the home.

In a recent critical review of this subject, Clarke and Clarke (11) have classified forms of deprivation in terms of the contributing environmental disorders. The major types include social isolation, cruelty and neglect, institutional upbringing, adverse child-rearing practices (less severe than "cruelty and neglect" and within the bounds of social acceptability), separation experiences, and socioeconomic deprivation. These are ranked in order of the severity of the effects to be expected from each of these types. When the cases discussed in this paper are analyzed for the presence or absence of each of these factors, it is seen that each clinical situation is a composite of several or all of them, varying in its total effect with the proportionate contribution of each. It would seem, too, that categorization of the more subtle differences in the emotional dynamics of child-rearing (all of which would fall under "adverse child-rearing practices") would be important in approaching this problem constructively.

Factors Affecting Susceptibility to Deprivation   As is true with all other forms of human disease, there are considerable individual differences in susceptibility to the effects of deprivation. Even in the most miasmal and monotonous of institutions, there were some hardy and resilient infants who did not develop the usual stigmata of deprivation. This could be explained by the supposition that there were inherited "constitutional" differences in vulnerability, and there is little reason to question the importance of such individual differences (as ill-defined as they are) in determining the response of any child to deprivational experiences. The duration and the intensity of these experiences is also a major influence on the severity of the outcome. Previous experience, as it affects the physical and emotional well-being of the child, is a factor of certain importance. The age at which the deprivation occurs is a most critical variable in determining the severity of the effects.

The gravest effects of separation are seen between the ages of three months and two years, and then gradually decrease in severity until the age of seven or eight when the child is able to tolerate long periods of separation without any lasting major damage to personality structure (8). The same can probably be said for forms of deprivation other than physical separation. In psychoanalytic terms, this most critical period (three months to two years) of psychic organization corresponds to the time of development of the ego, and to some extent, the superego, the success of which depends on the satisfactory establishment of a relationship with a clearly identified person—ordinarily the mother (8). Clarke and Clarke (11) seem to have similar meaning when they describe this vulnerable period of infancy and early childhood as the period of "perceptual and conceptual rigidity." This rigidity is felt to be a function of immature neural mechanisms whose rate of maturation is largely determined by the availability of "enriching" external stimulation.

Development of Current Ideas About Psychodynamics of Mother-Infant Relationship   With the support of such clinical observations as we have previously described, it can be said with fair certainty, then, that there are aspects of maternal function, above and beyond simple provision of adequate nutrients and protection from environmental extremes, which are essential for the normal growth and development of the human infant. It is generally accepted that the interests of the infant are best served by "a warm, intimate, and continuous relationship with his mother (or mother substitute) in which both find satisfaction and enjoyment" (8). Until recently, however, there has been little systematic investigation into the mechanisms by which the developing infant and his mother react to each other so as to create such a satisfactory relationship.

It was characteristic of mid-nineteenth century biological thought that infant behavior and emotional responses were held to be entirely instinctual phenomena, inherited products of natural selection, just as were the physical characteristics of the species. The atavistic concept is manifest in the suggestion of Charles Darwin himself that "fears of children, which are quite independent of experience, are the inherited effects of real dangers and abject superstitions during ancient savage times" (32).

The advent of psychoanalytic theory of personality development, however, was implemental in shifting interest toward the earliest perceptual experiences of the infant as the "foundation stone of his personality," and toward the basic role of the mother as the provider of these experiences (33). Despite much disagreement about the mechanisms involved, the theoretical basis lies in the concept of infantile sexuality, in which infant behavior is felt to be guided by an amorphous, undifferentiated body of pleasure seeking impulses (the id), rather than by any evolved pattern of instincts having survival value for the species. According to these principles, the early infant-mother attachment is a product of repeated gratification of physiologic needs, combined with stimulation of erotogenic (oral, in this case) zones. This attachment has been called the "libidinal cathexis" and has been thought to be the result of the "blissful experience of satisfaction and relief" (33), with the general implication that the needs of the infant for contact and human relationships spring secondarily from the satisfaction of basic needs for food, warmth, and oral gratification.

Benedek's (34) concept of the mother and child as a symbiotic unit seems to be a product of this theory. She describes this symbiosis as a continuation of that which existed during gestation and which was interrupted only briefly during parturition. The rhythmic and repetitive gratification of the infant's physiologic needs by the mother lead to the "development of confidence," upon which depends the satisfactory development of the ego and the

physical and emotional thriving of the infant. This normal interaction between mother and child is reciprocal and self-propagating,
in that the infant "feeds back" to the mother in emotional gratification what he receives from her in care, and, in so doing, main-
tains and increases her effectiveness as a mother. Here again, the
basic tenet is that the infant's tie to his mother figure is learned,
as a result of her repeated responses to his need for food.

In more recent years, however, the idea has gained more respect, among psychoanalysts as well as non-analytic psychologists,
that the need for an early attachment to a mother may be, to some
extent, an instinctual phenomenon, rather than one which is purely
acquired (33). Ribble (35), for instance, postulated that the infant
had an inborn "stimulus hunger" for certain specific modalities,
which included gentle touch and body contact, body position and
kinesthetic stimulation, and sound, particularly the soft sounds of
the human voice. These stimuli were transmitted to the infant
through the "whole gamut of small acts by means of which an emotionally healthy mother consistently shows her love for her child."
Bowlby (33) now proposes that the human infant is born with a
species-specific pattern of instinctual responses, which include
clinging, sucking, following, crying, and smiling. These are all
instincts which have survival value for the human infant, and their
existence is a product of natural selection. This author believes
that the primary function of the mother figure is one of integrating
these instinctual responses into a more complex pattern of "attachment behavior," and that the effects of maternal deprivation result
from interference with this integrating function. The clinging and
following instincts are given greater importance than some of the
others, such as sucking, for instance, which can apparently be dis-
placed more easily.

Observations of primate mother-infant behavior have con-
tributed a great deal, and, of these, Harlow's (36-39) investigations
of the infant-mother affectional system in macaque monkeys has
been outstanding. His work has shown clearly that contact-comfort
and clinging are the primary factors in the establishment of the
bond of affection between the infant monkey and his mother, and
that feeding, warmth, rocking, and visual and auditory stimuli have
only a supplemental role in the initiation and maintenance of this

bond. Strong and durable affectional ties were established by inanimate surrogate "mothers" of terry cloth who provided contact-comfort, and not by wire "mothers," even when the latter were the providers of food and warmth.

In the earlier phases of these investigations, it appeared that the cloth surrogate might be a perfectly satisfactory, or even superior, substitute for monkey mothers. As the surrogate-reared monkeys grew into adolescence, however, they began to show apathy, bizarre stereotyped reactions, and inappropriate sexual and social behavior. This was called "the non-social syndrome," and was similar in many ways to the behavior of children and adolescents who have had severe deprivation in infancy and early childhood. The behavioral and emotional development of these monkeys seemed to have been arrested at the level of the infant-mother (contact and clinging) affectional bond, a level of development which did not serve the subject well in the world of adult monkeys, and which certainly did not have value for the survival of the species.

The introduction of play experience with other young monkeys did not fully correct the inadequate social behavior of the surrogate-reared monkeys. There seems to be incontestable evidence, then, that mother-infant affection, and other maternal functions, too complex and too species specific to be provided by any other than a real monkey mother, are necessary for the attainment of normal behavior in the adolescent and adult animals. Although these mother-infant functions have not yet been reduced to such simple variables as the infant-mother affectional system, there is good reason to expect that continued research of this sort will do so, and that these investigations will continue to have important application in the study of human behavior.

Inborn behavioral characteristics in the infant may also be important in determining the character of these affectional bonds between mother and infant. Benedek (3, 34) has discussed the role of the infant in this regard, and Brazelton (40) has recently reported an instance in which a "deficit in responsiveness" on the part of a newborn seemed to be the major etiologic factor in the establishment of an unhappy relationship between mother and infant.

Deprivation and Growth   There are several ways in which the circumstances of infant deprivation might interfere with anabolic
activity and the nutritional status of the child. First and most
obvious would be an actual failure, deliberate or otherwise, by
the parents to provide adequate calories, protein or other essential
nutrients. The degree to which this occurs in any given situation
is difficult to ascertain or to control. There is evidence that this
plays a role in three of the cases presented here. The others were
said to have been provided adequate diets, although, of course,
none of the dietary histories was above suspicion.

A reduction in appetite and feeding activity, concomitant with
the emotional depression and lassitude seen in the deprivation
syndrome, might also be a factor of importance. It is becoming
evident that infant nutrition is a complex product of cultural and
emotional, as well as biochemical, factors (41, 42). In Uganda,
for instance, the youngest child is immediately sent away to a
relative when a new sibling is born. Geber and Dean (43) think
that the emotional effects of this sudden separation from mother
are as important in the etiology of kwashiorkor as is the actual
scarcity of dietary protein. These behavioral changes (depression,
apathy, and anorexia) resulting from acute maternal deprivation
may be the primary events which then, in a society which requires
aggressive foraging to acquire adequate protein, may lead to or
accentuate the state of malnutrition. The presence of the mother
was also noted by these authors to have a favorable effect on the
rate of recovery.

Another possibility is that changes in intestinal motility and
rates of absorption might be altered in these children in such a
way as to prevent efficient assimilation of ingested nutrients. The
relationship between the central nervous system, emotions, and
gastrointestinal function is certainly supported by a vast amount
of clinical and experimental data, beginning with the historic
collaboration of Dr. Beaumont and his patient, Aléxis St. Mar-
tin, (44). Of particular pertinence are the studies by Engel,
Reichsman, and Segal (45) of their infant female patient with
esophageal atresia and gastric fistula. These investigators found
that "gastric secretion was intimately integrated with the total

behavioral activity" of the infant. There was a marked reduction of gastric hydrochloric acid production when the child was depressed and withdrawn, and an increase during rage, oral activity, or any activity related to external objects.

Disturbances of gastrointestinal function (vomiting, diarrhea, and constipation) are prominent in the clinical histories of the patients presented in this paper. One child (Case 2), while still showing the behavioral features of "anaclitic depression," absorbed only 4.2 per cent of an administered dose of d-xylose. This test has not been repeated, but his rapid weight gain and linear growth, and normal stools, since his placement in the foster home, would seem to weigh against the presence of any significant malabsorbtion now.

A fourth possible explanation is that emotional disturbances of the magnitude often seen in deprived infants might have a direct effect on intermediary metabolism in such a way as to alter the rates of anabolic processes. This might occur through cortical-hypothalamic-hypophyseal pathways involving known endocrine systems, or through hormonal, neural or neurohumoral mechanisms yet to be defined. There is certainly good evidence that the production and release of anterior pituitary hormones (FSH, LH, TSH, ACTH, and probably prolactin) are influenced in a major way by hypothalamic centers. These centers are, in turn, probably recipients of pathways from higher neural centers, particularly the limbic cortex and amygdaloid nuclei, and also the habenular region, frontal cortex, hippocampus, and mesencephalic reticular formation (46-48).

It is interesting that, in addition to its neuroendocrine functions, the limbic cortex is also felt to be the locus of emotional feeling and behavior (49), so that clinical observations of the effect of emotions on lactation, cyclic sexual functions, and adrenocortical activity are acquiring a demonstrable anatomic basis. It may also be that more direct neural influences on intermediary metabolism may be important in determining growth rates. For example, it has been shown that emotional stress, probably through the sympathetic nervous system, causes an increased rate of free fatty acid mobilization from depots (50). Growth being an endergonic process, it would seem reasonable to suspect that anabolic reactions might be affected by any such neural influences on the availability of the primary substrates for cellular energy production. Here again, the anatomic proximity of the autonomic centers and the "emotion centers" in the limbic system gives support to these observed associations.

Finally, recent experiments have demonstrated a direct effect of certain hypothalamic areas on growth, which is independent of any observed hormonal or metabolic changes. Reichlin (51) has observed that experimental damage to the anterior half of the median eminence of the rat hypothalamus produces retardation of linear growth, weight gain, and tibial length, and that this is not corrected by the administration of thyroxin, testosterone, corticosterone, desoxycorticosterone acetate, pitressin, or by increased food intake. The hypothesis that this is the result of a decreased production of pituitary growth hormone has been suggested but not proven.

Recorded clinical observations, too, have supported such a relationship between disturbed emotional states and decreased growth rates. We have already mentioned the earlier studies of the institutional syndrome, in which were described "failure to thrive" and extreme growth retardation despite "good food and meticulous medical care" (20, 21). Talbot, Sobel, and co-workers (52) described a group of twenty-one calorically undernourished dwarfs, who did not respond to the provision of an adequate diet. It was found that the majority of these children were emotionally disturbed, because of maternal rejection, hostile attitudes on the part of the parents, or because of family disruption. There was true poverty in only three cases. In some of these children, correction of the emotional difficulties led to rapid acceleration of growth; in others, there was unexplained failure to resume growth at normal rates, even after assured correction of all dietary inadequacies.

Fried and Mayer (53) carefully followed the growth patterns of children in a metropolitan children's home, and found a striking correlation between growth rates and emotional adjustment. They observed that caloric supplementation did not induce return of normal growth until the emotional disorder had been corrected. Binning (54), in a similar study of 800 Saskatoon school children, found that deviations from the normal rates of growth were related more often to events which produced emotional disturbances than to physical illnesses. Widdowson (55) has described a study of weight gain among children in two German orphanages, in which the nutritional factors were carefully controlled. The children who received dietary supplements gained less weight than the group remaining on basic rations—a fact which was unexplained until it was found that the supervisor of the first orphanage was harsh and unsympathetic, and subjected her charges to a great deal of unnecessary harassment.

Bransby and co-workers (56) did longitudinal growth studies of 3,000 English school children, and attempted to correlate growth status with the following factors: social and emotional stability within the home, the economic status of the family, and the size of the family. There were significant height and weight differences in favor of the children from the smaller families and from families of higher economic standing, but by far the most striking differences were found in the first category, in which the children had been grouped according to the quality of the social and emotional environment within the family.

Factors Effecting Reversibility of Environmentally Produced Growth Retardation   Although the periods of observation are not long enough to permit any firm conclusions, it is interesting that the children described here showed much variability in the rapidity with which they regained age-norms for height, weight, and bone-age, after they had been placed in more favorable environments. It is certainly possible that this variability is related in some degree to genetic differences between these children. It might be also, however, that these long term effects represent a permanent impairment of the ability to grow, resulting from the deprivation in early childhood, and that differences in degree might be related to the severity and duration of the environmental disturbances. These effects, then, would be analogous to the persistent lag in intellectual and emotional development previously mentioned.

There have been few anthropometric studies concerned with

the effects of early environment on growth in later childhood and adolescence. Secular increases in stature have been held by many to be a result of improved child care and nutrition (27), and Wolff (57), in 1935, described a study of a large number of German school children who had been born during the 1917-1919 period of food shortage. This group of children still had a significant growth deficit on entering school, when compared to children born earlier than 1917 or later than 1919. This author felt that growth, although "primarily a function of innate constitution," could be modified considerably by deprivation in utero or in infancy, and agreed that the secular increases in size were attributable to the general improvement in social and economic conditions.

Among experimental biologists, however, there had been considerable interest in this problem since the early part of the century. The point in question was whether the capacity to grow, the "wachstumfähigkeit," was a property only of young cells, which inevitably declined and was lost with age, or whether this growth potential remained with the organism until exercised. Aron (58), in 1910, concluded, from his experiments with dogs, that these animals retained their growth capacity, after inhibition of growth throughout early life, only if the growth inhibition were discontinued prior to the end of the normal growing age. When inhibition was extended through adolescence the capacity to grow was lost.

Osborne and Mendel (59), on the other hand, in a series of experiments with rats, suppressed growth by various dietary means for periods of time considerably greater than the normal 335 day growth period, and found that, when the suppression was released, the animals had an acceleration of growth which allowed them to reach normal size. Their experiments were begun after weaning, however, and the final weights and lengths of their animals were not closely compared with those of controls. Jackson (60) subjected weanling rats to a degree of caloric undernutrition which maintained their body weights at about 50 gm. for fifteen weeks. These animals, too, had a remarkable acceleration of growth when a free diet was resumed. Despite this, they never

reached the weights of the controls, the latter group being sixteen per cent heavier than the test animals at sixty weeks of age.

Clarke and Smith (61) produced growth retardation in thirty-
five day old rats by means of low salt diets as well as by caloric
deprivation. When stunting was done for three weeks the animals
fully regained normal growth; when experimental conditions were
continued for six and twelve week periods, however, permanent
growth deficits resulted, the degree of which was in proportion
to the length of deprivation. Barnes, Sperling, and McCay (62)
measured tibial lengths in rats whose growth had been retarded
by restricted diets for varying periods, and found that, although
there was a growth spurt after realimentation, none of the tibiae
of the retarded growth rats achieved final lengths as great as those
of the controls. Here again, the deficit was in proportion to the
length of the caloric deprivation. In similar experiments, Saxton
and Silberberg (63) found that some capacity for "rebound"
growth remained in animals who had been subject to nutritional
retardation for as long as 1,150 days, but that the degree of growth
attainable after realimentations was in inverse proportion to the
duration of the growth suppression.* It should be noted that
all of the experiments mentioned above were done with animals
past the weaning period. There has been more recent evidence
that nutritional factors may have much greater long term effects
when they are allowed to operate at an earlier period of life(64).
Kennedy (65) has shown that rats from small litters are significantly larger throughout their life spans than are rats from larger
litters. It seems that, in this species, the first week of life is critical
in determining future rates of growth, and that differences in
weight at the end of the first week or ten days bear a direct relationship to future food intake and adult weight. The mechanism
is obscure; there is no evidence that this phenomenon is under
either hypothalamic or hormonal control.

---

*Although not pertinent to the present discussion, it must be mentioned that
these experiments also show that the life span of the rat is significantly prolonged by
this undernutrition, primarily because of the slower development of the common
degenerative changes, and because of the later appearance and reduced incidence of
tumors. Similar beneficial effects of undernutrition have been noted in other animals.
This certainly presents a challenge to the widely held concept that maximal growth
and optimal growth are identical (66).

In summary, experimental work over the past half century has shown that, despite a remarkable mammalian capacity for "rebound" from prolonged periods of growth stunting, unfavorable environmental factors, which are of sufficient intensity to delay growth in early life, may have long term effects which persist despite full correction of the environmental changes. The severity of these effects certainly seems to be related to the duration and intensity of the deprivation, which, in these experiments, has been one of total calories, protein, of other essential nutritional factors. The age of the animal is also an important variable, and there is now evidence that there may be a specific and very sensitive response to these environmental changes when they occur very early in the life of the animal.

Deprivation and Epiphyseal Maturation   Retardation of osseous maturation was a prominent finding in these cases. Three of these children had retardation of bone-age which was even greater than that of height-age. There were no anomalies of ossification such as epiphyseal dysgenesis or the pseudo-epiphyses and notching described by Snodgrasse and his associates (5). Very prominent however, were the dense, thin, transverse lines at the ends of the long bones. Although followup data is not adequate in all cases, there has seemed to be an early acceleration of epiphyseal maturation in the younger children (Cases 2, 3, 5, and 6) after hospitalization and foster home placement. This coincided in time with the early gains in rate of weight-gain and linear growth, but was less pronounced than those increases. Of those two children who were followed for longer periods, one (Case 3) had normal bone age by the age of eight, but the other (Case 4) did not regain the norm for his age until late puberty, at fourteen.

Observations of the rates of appearance, changes in size and shape, and fusion of various skeletal centers have, for the past half century, been of great value in the study of both normal and deviant patterns of growth in infants, children and adolescents. Although other centers must be examined in specific situations, the development of the skeleton of the hand and wrist has been most carefully documented, and is most widely used as an indi-

cator of osseous maturity in clinical and anthropometric investigations (4, 27). The importance of the endocrine system in control of rates of bone maturation became apparent as the result
of observations in three major areas. These included the close
association between the degree of sexual maturity and the state of
epiphyseal development during adolescence, the severe delay in
bone development found in hypothyroidism and panhypopitui-
tarism and the acceleration seen in adrenal virilism and the various types of precocious puberty, and, finally, the observed effects
of androgens and estrogens on bone age when used therapeutically
in the growing child.

These observations have, in the past, tended to foster the
widely held impression that epiphyseal maturation is purely a
function of hormonal action, and that severe alterations in the
rate of this process are pathognomonic of a specific endocri-
nopathy. More recent studies of growth disorders, however, utiliz-
ing newer and more exact techniques for measuring endocrine
functions, have shown this to be far from true. Mellman and
his associates (67), in fact, have reported that only 30 per cent of
their patients with skeletal retardation had true "endocrine disease," even though this series consisted of referrals to an endocrine
clinic, and was thus biased in that direction.

It now appears that there are many factors, both genetic and
environmental, which affect the rate of epiphyseal maturation as
they affect the growth rate in general, often producing extreme
deviations from normal in the absence of any deficiency of the
known hormonal substances. Francis (68) stated that skeletal
retardation was more sensitive than any of the other parameters
of growth and development, as an indicator of the effects of disease in infancy. Dreizen, *et al.* (6) have shown that chronic undernutrition produces retardation of skeletal maturation, assymetrical
patterns of ossification, anomalies such as notching and pseudo-
epiphyses, and delayed fusion of epiphyses in late adolescence.
These workers also found that the degree and rapidity of the response to dietary supplementation with protein decreased as the
child grew older. Retardation of bone development in protein
malnutrition has been reported by Gopalan (69) in India and by

Jones and Dean (70) in Uganda. Talbot and co-workers (52) described significant retardation of bone age in children with chronic
undernutrition related to emotional disturbances.

Animal experiments have indicated that epiphyseal development may lag somewhat behind changes in body weight and body
length which occur with changes in the level of nutrition (71).
This is in agreement with the findings in the cases reported here.
Of particular pertinence to this discussion are the findings of
Nissen and Riesen (72), who studied the effects of various environmental factors on rates of ossification in young chimpanzees.
Among the conditions which caused retardation of bone-age in
these animals were light-deprivation during infancy, and restriction of the opportunity to grasp and other tactual experience.

Although the alterations in rates of ossification of the round
bones (carpals and tarsals) and the epiphyses are more obvious, it
is also reasonable to expect that adverse environmental circumstances might effect the metabolism of the long bones, particularly
in the metaphyseal areas where bone lengthening occurs. The
fact that deprived children have impaired linear growth is, of
course, prima facie evidence that this does happen. More specific
radiological evidence may be provided by lines of increased density
at the ends of the long bones, which are called "scars of interrupted
growth" by Greulich and Pyle (4). These are said to represent a
temporary imbalance between rates of calcification and linear bone
growth, in which mineralization occurs at its original rate even
though bone lengthening has been slowed by illness, malnutrition
or other causes. Such lines were found to be very common among
the undernourished children studied by Dreizen and his associates
(6), and in the Uganda children with kwashiorkor by Jones and
Dean (70). A large number of the children of Hiroshima and Naga-
saki were found years later to have dense transverse lines in their
long bones, whose time of formation would have corresponded
closely to that of the atomic bombings (4). It should be pointed
out, however, that Caffey (73) doubts that growth retardation is
always essential to the production of these lines, and states that they
may occur in a fair number of normal children.

Mention should be made of the unusual relationship between

skeletal age and sexual maturation which was seen in one of these patients (Case 4). It is generally accepted that the maturation of the skeleton has a specific and intimate relationship with the maturation of the reproductive system, and, in turn, to the somatic changes of puberty (4, 21). This relationship has been quite dependable except in such definite endocrine disorders as precocious puberty and hypopituitarism. In this patient, however, who had no detectable hormonal abnormality, there was definite pubertal testicular enlargement at a time when the skeletal age was five years (the chronological age being 11 years), and puberty was well advanced when the bone age was seven and one-half years (Figs. 10-12). Whether or not this unusual lag in epiphyseal development is related to the earlier deprivation remains a matter for conjecture.

[References at end of Chap. V]

Chapter 4

> *Lennie's lip quivered and tears started in his eyes. "Aw Lennie!" George put his hand on Lennie's shoulder. "I ain't takin' it away jus' for meanness. That mouse ain't fresh, Lennie; and besides, you've broke it pettin' it. You get another mouse that's fresh and I'll let you keep it a little while. . . . Your Aunt Clara give you a rubber mouse and you wouldn't have nothing to do with it."*
>
> *"It wasn't no good to pet," said Lennie.*
>
>

JOHN STEINBECK,
Of Mice and Men, Chap. 1, 1937
>

Case Histories of Children with Maternal Deprivation and Growth Retardation

Case 1

History   D.S., a fifteen month old girl, was first admitted to St. Joseph's Hospital, Syracuse, on April 4, 1955, for investigation of growth failure and constipation. She had been born at term, weighing 5 lbs. 1 oz. (2.3 kg.), after a pregnancy complicated by rupture of the membranes in the second trimester, and by pre-eclampsia. There was meconium staining at birth, but no further neonatal difficulties developed, and the baby was sent home at one week of age. During the first month, she vomited often after feedings and had watery stools as often as fifteen to twenty times daily. After several formula changes, this cleared, and thereafter she was said to have had an excellent, almost ravenous appetite. Solid foods were begun early and taken well. Oleum percomorphum and a standard vitamin preparation were given, 0.6 cc. of each daily. Despite this apparently adequate intake, the child failed to gain weight and exhibited lethargic behavior, sleeping sixteen to eighteen hours daily. She had become progressively more constipated, to the point of having one hard stool weekly. She smiled at one month of age, sat at six months, and stood with support at ten months. Motor activity had decreased markedly during the months prior to admission, and she had not talked. There had been a persistent respiratory infection, with cough and wheezing, for three months before admission. Her weight three months before admission had been 12 lbs. (5.4 kg.), 2 lbs. more than the admission weight.

Family History The mother, twenty-one, was about five feet tall and in good health. Her own childhood had been marked by rejection and extreme domestic instability. The father was twenty-six, 5' 9" tall, and was said to have "ulcers and malaria." He was described as an "inadequate person" who worked only sporadically, and was an alcoholic. There was a sister, twenty-six months old, who weighed twenty-four pounds, and was thirty-four inches tall. The father disclaimed the patient as his own child, and the mother was said to have a "violent hatred" of her. She was kept, isolated and unattended, in a dark room, and was removed only to be fed perfunctorily. There was no evidence of physical trauma, however, prior to the first admission.

Physical Findings This fifteen month old girl was 58 cm. in height (height-age* three months) and weighed 4.4 kg. The head circumference was 40 cm. She appeared much less mature than her actual age, was malnourished and extremely retarded in growth. She was very lethargic and withdrawn, and ignored the examiner. Her skin was dry, with crusted excoriations over the face and diaper area. The anterior fontanelle was open. There were four upper and two lower incisors. Examination of the ears, nose, throat, heart and lungs revealed no abnormalities. The abdomen was soft, the liver being palpable 1.5 cm. below the costal margin.

---

*Height-age = determined from the 50th percentile of Stuart's developmental chart.

The extremities were thin and poorly muscled. There were no neurological abnormalities.

Laboratory Data   The peripheral blood and urine were normal. The fasting blood sugar was 61 mg. per cent, and the two hour post-carbohydrate blood sugar 67 mg. per cent. The blood non-protein nitrogen was 31 mg. per cent. There was no steatorrhea, and trypsin was present in the stool through a 1:200 dilution. There was normal lipiodol absorption. The urinary amino acid nitrogen excretion was 400 mg. in twenty-four hours.

Roentgenographic Findings   Films of the skull and chest were normal. Hand and wrist films indicated a bone-age of six months. The hips, knees, shoulders and feet, however, showed maturation approximating a twelve month level. There were prominent transverse lines of growth arrest at the ends of the long bones. Urograms were normal.

Course   During the hospitalization, great improvement occurred in all aspects of development. The diet was taken eagerly, and there was a weight gain of more than three pounds in four weeks. The skin lesions healed rapidly. Bowel function was normal. The most striking change occurred in her affect and social responsiveness; her cringing, fearful, apathetic attitude disappeared quickly. She became outgoing, friendly and more self-assertive. There was acceleration in motor development, and she began to talk for the first time.

She was discharged on May 6, 1955, although the mother was reluctant to take her home. The original pattern of rejection and isolation was resumed, but, instead of responding in her previous passive, apathetic manner, the child now protested this treatment by crying loudly and showing temper. The mother reacted to this new behavior by abusing the child physically, and, on May 23, 1955, she was found by a social worker "in a bruised and malnourished state," and was rehospitalized. Again she responded well to the attention of the nursing staff, gained weight rapidly and seemed happy.

At this point, the parents agreed to foster home placement for the child, and accepted long-term psychiatric therapy for themselves. The child did well in her new environment. The sharp upswing in her growth velocity continued for about a year, although she remained in the lower percentiles in later years (Fig. 1.).

Two years later she weighed 28¼ pounds (12.8 kg.) and was 35 inches (88 cm.) in height. She improved, as well, in her ability to form interpersonal relationships, although the attending social worker continued to note a lack of depth and spontaneity of affect. Considerable improvement having been brought about in the family situation, she was returned to her parents at the age of five. She has now begun school, and is reported to be doing well.

Case 2

History H.C., a three year old boy, was admitted to the Syracuse Memorial Hospital on September 8, 1960 (his fourth admission) for investigation of his extreme retardation of growth and development. His birth weight was 7 lbs. 3 oz. (3.2 kg.) and he was said to have been an eager feeder from early infancy. Despite his good intake, he failed to gain satisfactorily and was admitted for study at the age of six months. He weighed 12 lbs (5.5 kg.) at that time, and had a generalized impetiginous rash. No specific causes for his "failure to thrive" were found, but maternal deprivation was suspected at that time. The diet was carefully supervised, and intake, as best could be determined, was adequate. Rumination was reported occasionally. He was rehospitalized at eight months of age, weighing 12 lbs., 14 oz. (5.9 kg.). At this time he was more active, and had two teeth. The hemoglobin was 9.9 gm. per cent, and urograms were normal. He gained weight rapidly while in the hospital, weighing 13 lbs., 10 oz. (6 kg.) on discharge. After this, however, the growth rate again declined. The boy was admitted for the third time at the age of fifteen months, weighing 14 lbs., 15 oz. (6.8 kg.), and measuring 29 inches (72.5 cm.) in length. Despite his malnourished appearance, his mother insisted that his appetite was voracious and food intake allegedly adequate—one quart of evaporated milk formula daily, a good variety of solid foods, and multivitamins.

At this time, the hemoglobin was 11.8 gm. per cent, the stool contained trypsin to a 1:240 dilution, and did not contain excess fat or starch. Bone-age was between three and six months. Six teeth were present. He did not sit or stand at this time, and speech was limited to "babbling." There was again rapid weight gain in the hospital, and he was discharged to the mother's care, but under the surveillance of a welfare agency. One month later, he weighed 18 lbs., 4 oz. (8.3 kg.). There was no further weight gain despite the mother's insistence that the prescribed diet had been provided and consumed. His appetite was still said to be voracious, although he continued to practice regurgitation and reswallowing often. He was usually constipated but had frequent isolated episodes of diarrhea and many respiratory infections. He began to crawl and to take steps with support at two years of age. At two and one-half, he had begun to feed himself with his fingers, and said a few single words. He was not toilet trained.

During this period, the paternal grandmother had reported the mother to the domestic court for neglecting her children, and blamed this for the failure to thrive on the part of this patient. He was readmitted (fourth admission) for further studies prior to foster home placement.

Family History The mother was twenty-one and in good health. The father was twenty-six, well, with a questionable history of "rickets" during infancy. A sister, four, and a brother, seven months, were of normal size.

The mother had been deserted by her own mother at the age of four. At the age of seventeen she became pregnant, and was placed in a detention home by her father. She was married one year later, but the marriage was described as being "on the rocks" after six months.

The father worked only occasionally, was away from home a great deal, and was said to have had several extra-marital affairs. He threatened his wife with violence when she mentioned taking any legal action against this behavior. The family had recently been evicted from their home for failure to pay the rent. During this last hospitalization, it was noted that the mother seemed quite detached and emotionless in her relationship to the patient.

She visited very rarely, showed no interest in taking him home, and, in fact, was quite happy to have him placed in a foster home. She admitted that he was a great source of annoyance to her, and was convinced that "he hates us."

Physical Findings This was a dull, apathetic boy of three years (Fig. 5) who weighed 15 lbs. 6 oz. (7 kg.) and was 29¼ inches (72.5 cm.) in length. The head circumference was 18¾ inches (47 cm.), normal for age twelve months, and the upper segment/lower segment ratio was 1.34, normal for thirty-six months. He appeared malnourished and more infantile than he should have been for his actual age. He was extremely withdrawn and inactive, and speech was limited to unintelligible single words. The skin was pale, dry, mottled, but warm. There was little subcutaneous fat. The eyes, ears, nose, and throat were normal. All deciduous teeth were present. The chest was clear and the heart normal. The abdomen was protuberant, and a soft liver edge was palpable two cm. below the costal margin. The genitalia were normal except for an excoriated diaper rash. The extremities were thin and wasted, but there was normal movement at all joints and tendon reflexes were present symmetrically. Muscle tone was moderately decreased.

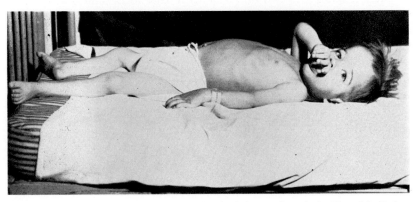

Fig. 5. Patient H.C. (Case 2) on fourth admission to hospital. Note his listless appearance, and "frog-leg" position. His mother appeared detached and emotionless in relation to him. With a chronological age of three years, he had a bone age of fifteen months.

Laboratory Data   On admission, the hemoglobin was 8.7 gm. per cent, reticulocytes 1.4 per cent. Three weeks later, after iron therapy, the hemoglobin was 10.5 gm. per cent, the reticulocytes 3 per cent. Urinalyses were normal, with specific gravities as high as 1.021. Occult blood was found in one stool specimen, but others were negative. Ova and parasites were absent, and there was no steatorrhea or other abnormality of the stool suggesting malabsorption. Four and two-tenths per cent of an administered dose of d-xylose was excreted in the urine in five hours. The blood urea nitrogen was 25 per cent and 13 per cent on two occasions. The serum calcium was 9.3 mg. per cent, the serum inorganic phosphorus 5.3 mg. per cent, and the alkaline phosphatase 3.5 Bessey-Lowry units. The serum iron was 61 micrograms per cent, and the iron-binding capacity 137 micrograms per cent. The serum protein-bound iodine was 4.9 micrograms per cent. The total serum proteins were 6.6 with an albumin-globulin ratio of 5.1/1.5, and 7.0 with a ratio of 4.6/2.4. The sweat chloride was 31 meq/liter and the sweat sodium 22 meq/liter. Serum sodium and potassium concentrations were normal.

Roentgenographic Findings   The carpal-phalangeal bone age was fifteen months. There were three transverse lines of growth arrest in each distal radius. The chest film and intravenous urograms were normal.

Course   As previously, there was rapid weight gain in the hospital, an increase of more than six pounds in six weeks. There was an equally pronounced change in his intellectual and motor status. He became interested in his surroundings, enjoyed the attention given him by the nursing staff, and was soon walking with support. He was placed in a supervised foster home by the welfare department.

When seen four months later, he weighed thirty-five pounds (16 kg.) and was 33 inches (82.5 cm). tall (Figs. 6 and 7). He was walking well alone and was talking, with a large vocabulary and three or four word sentences. He was described by the foster mother as being happy and outgoing. He seemed quite attached to his foster mother, and yet was "independent," insisting on

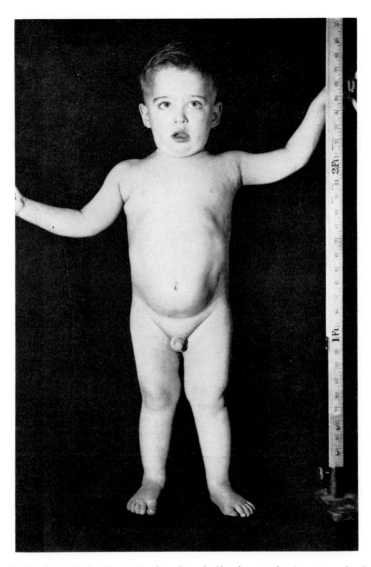

Fig. 6. Patient H.C. (Case 2) after hospitalization and placement in foster home. The improvement in this child's nutrition in a few months makes it difficult to recognize him as the same boy shown in Figure 5.

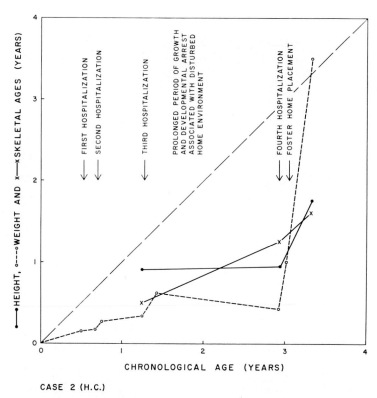

CASE 2 (H.C.)

Fig. 7. Growth chart of patient H.C. (Case 2). The wasting away of this boy is demonstrated graphically here, showing his body weight to be less at three years of age than at eighteen months. His response to the fourth hospitalization was dramatic, with an increase of more than six pounds in six weeks. The slope of his weight gain curve was maintained in the foster home, with the result that his weight quickly reached the 50th percentile for his age. Note, however, that osseous development and linear growth had not responded in so rapid a manner to the improvement in home environment.

being left to roam and explore, and on being allowed to dress himself. Toilet-training had been accomplished without difficulty within three weeks. His appetite had remained excellent, and there had been no diarrhea or steatorrhea.

Case 3

History C.W., a thirteen and one-half month old girl, was admitted to the Syracuse Memorial Hospital on November 5, 1953, with a history of "doing poorly" since early infancy. She had been born at term, weighing 5 lbs. 13 oz. (2.6 kg.). She had been breast-fed for the first few days, then put on an evaporated milk formula. which was changed on several occasions because of vomiting. For the first two months of life, however, the infant apparently did well. During this time, she was held by her mother for feeding, and received a good deal of personal attention from her. She was reported to have smiled and vocalized at two months of age. At about this time, the mother was advised by neighbor that she was "spoiling her child" by this attention. She then discontinued all physical contact or attention to the child which was not absolutely unavoidable. The bottle was propped for feeding and the child was left alone in her carriage during all of her waking hours. There was soon a pronounced reduction in activity and change in mood. The infant stopped smiling, looked down when anyone was near and refused to take or to hold toys. As related by the mother, the daily diet consisted of twelve ounces of whole milk, one egg, one jar each of strained fruits and vegetables, oatmeal, two ounces of orange juice, and one dropper full of oleum per-comorphum. She did not take the solid foods well, however, and these were offered only perfunctorily. During a few days prior to admission, listlessness and anorexia became even more pro-nounced.

Family History The whereabouts of the father, age forty-two, were unknown. He had recently been released from prison, and had a record of fifty-nine arrests. The mother, age forty, was mentally retarded, and required the constant supervision of wel-fare workers. Three older siblings had been adjudged neglected in 1939, and placed in foster homes. Another child had died in 1937, probably of malnutrition. Two other siblings and the mother were at this time boarded in a foster home by the welfare department. One of these siblings was said to have a speech and hearing defect, and both showed evidence of poor physical care.

Physical Findings The child weighed 10 lbs. (4.5 kg.) and was 27½ inches (58.75 cm.) in length (height-age 9 months). The head circumference was 16 in. (40 cm.), the body temperature

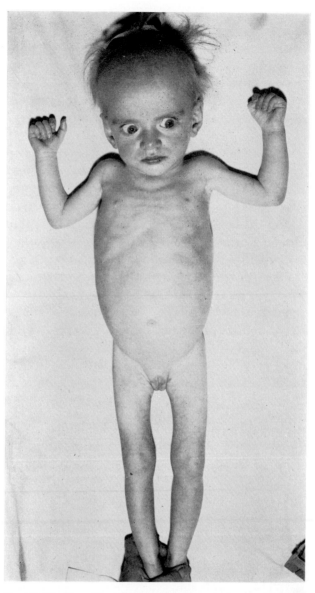

Fig. 8. Patient C.W. (Case 3) on admission to hospital at age thirteen and one-half months. She was extremely small (height-age nine months), and lay on her back without moving. Unless disturbed she made no sound. Her mentally retarded mother had been told by a neighbor that she was "spoiling" her child, so all attention and physical contact to this infant had been cut off. Although

⋙→

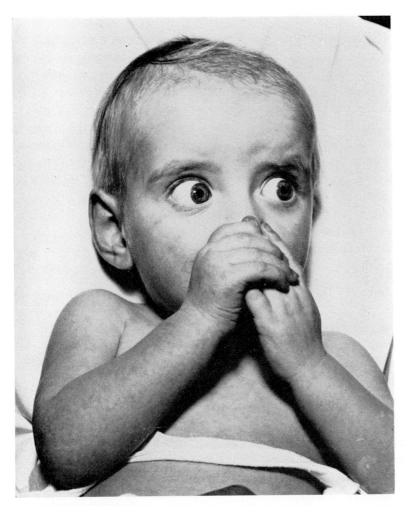

Fig. 9. Patient C.W. (Case 3) on admission to hospital—a close-up view. When left alone she usually assumed this position with her hands cupped over her face, and her legs drawn up. The constantly anxious expression on her face is demonstrated here and also in Figure 8.

she had smiled and cooed prior to this time, afterwards she developed progressive anorexia and listlessness. It is of interest to compare this reaction with that of the adult volunteer subjects described in Chapter 1, who developed a distaste for food during experimental sensory deprivation.

94.6°F. Respirations were ten to fifteen per minute and irregular. The pulse rate was 72 per minute. She was an extremely small, malnourished girl who lay, almost motionless, on her back with legs drawn up and with her hands cupped tightly over mouth and nose (Figs. 8 and 9). She cried when attempts were made to remove the hands from this position, but otherwise made no sound. There was an anxious facial expression. The hair was sparse. There was a mucoid nasal discharge. There were two upper and two lower incisors. The chest was clear and the heart normal. The abdomen was protuberant but soft. The liver edge was palpable two cm. below the right costal margin, but was felt to be normal. There were pustular lesions on the labia majora. The forearms, hands and feet were red and edematous. Muscle tone was poor; there was very little spontaneous movement of the extremities, and no attempts were made to roll over, sit, or stand.

Laboratory Data   The hemoglobin was 9.0 gm. per cent, later 11.5 gm. per cent. The white blood cell count was 8,800 per cubic mm., with a normal differential. Urinalyses were normal. The serum proteins were 4.8 gm. per cent. Other liver function studies were normal. The blood non-protein nitrogen was 40 mg. per cent, and the fasting blood sugar 80 mg. per cent. The stool contained trypsin and did not have excess fat or starch.

Roentgenographic Findings   The bone age on admission was six months. There was osteoporosis, and there were transverse lines of growth arrest in the long bones. Skull x-rays were normal, as were intravenous pyelograms. Contrast studies of the upper and lower gastrointestinal tract were normal. In the sixth month of hospitalization, at a chronological age of eighteen months, the bone age was nine months.

Course   There was continued apathy and failure to gain weight during the first three weeks of hospitalization. Most of the diagnostic studies mentioned above were done during this time. On November 28, twenty-three days after admission, a nurse was assigned to give the child special attention, to pick her up, carry her about, and to perform other such "mothering" functions as often as time permitted. Within a few days there was a noticeable increase in brightness of mood and activity. The infant began to vocalize, say "mama," and showed keen recognition and appreciation of her substitute "mother." There was a sharp increase in appetite and weight gain began (Fig. 10). Two months after her hospital admission she was smiling, sitting without support, and rolling from back to abdomen. She was described by this time as having "a very happy disposition." She began to creep during the fourth months in hospital, and a month later was able

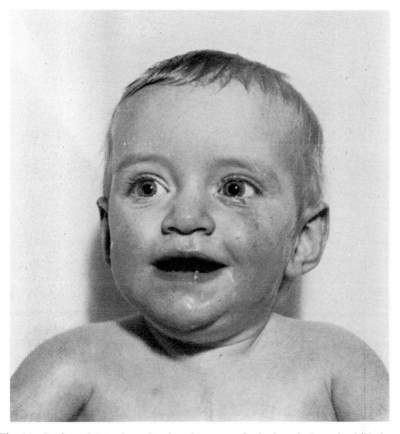

Fig. 10. Patient C.W. (Case 3) after four months in hospital, and after three months of "mothering" mostly by one nurse. Within a few days after this special attention was started the infant brightened up, began to say "mama" to her "mother," and ate much better. A few weeks later she was sitting without support, rolling over at will, and gaining weight rapidly.

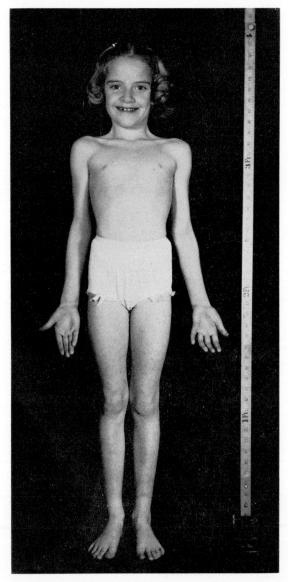

Fig. 11. Patient C.W. (Case 3) at eight years of age. She was doing well in the second grade of school, and living happily with foster parents. Her physical progress had been good, but psychological testing showed persistent abnormalities in personality structure. She was active and affectionate.

to pull to a standing position, and to propel herself in a "walker." On June 8, 1954, she was discharged to the care of a foster mother who had been selected by the welfare department. This proved to be a very satisfactory arrangement, and she continued to do quite well.

At the age of two years and three months her weight was 20 lbs. (9.1 kg.) and her bone age fifteen months. She was talking in sentences and had begun to walk. At the age of four years, two months, she weighed 31 lbs. (14.1 kg), continued to be happy and seemed to be developing normally. She was seen again at eight years of age, now very happily situated with another foster family. She was in the second grade and doing well. She had been well physically, was active, and described as being a happy and affecnate girl. Psychological testing, however, revealed persistent abnormalities in personality structure, and the I.Q. was in the dull normal range. Her weight at this time was 42 lbs. (19.1 kg.), her height 47⅛ inches (117.5 cm.), and her bone age seven years, six months (see Figs. 11 and 12).

Case 4

History R.A. was referred to this clinic in June, 1953, when six and one-half years old, for investigation of his retarded growth. He had weighed 5 lbs. 1 oz. (2.3 kg.) at birth, and was said to be a "seven month baby." He was sent home from the hospital at two weeks of age, and during the neonatal period was very difficult to feed. He refused the bottle, and had to be fed with a spoon until the cup was introduced at one month of age. Solid foods were begun early but not taken well. Early growth was felt to be satisfactory, and it was not until the age of about twenty months that his mother felt that growth "stopped." X-rays, taken at another hospital when the boy was four, revealed a bone age of approximately eighteen months (multiple centers). Films of the wrist at five and one-half years of age showed ossification at the two and one half year level. The parents were told at this time that he "might lack a growth hormone." Appetite was said to have improved in the year prior to this admission, and, as described, the diet was nutritionally adequate. He was said to be

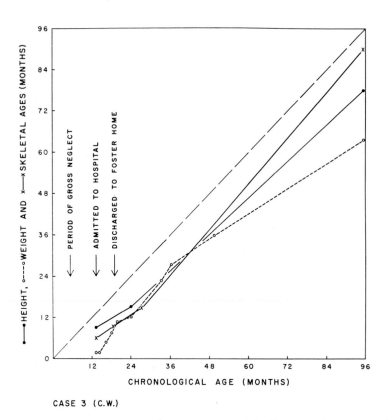

CASE 3 (C.W.)

Fig. 12. Growth chart of patient C.W. (Case 3). The disproportionate retardation of weight-age in this child gives graphic evidence that she can be classified as a "thin dwarf" (also supported by her appearance in Fig. 8). As early as 1947 Talbot, Sobel *et al.* (52) noted the association of the "thin dwarf" with those disturbances in family environment which we now term maternal deprivation. When first admitted to hospital at age thirteen and one-half months her bone age was six months. At age twenty-seven months her bone age was fifteen months. This is distinct retardation of osseous development. By age eight years her bone age was seven and one-half years (within the range of normal), which indicates that her osseous maturation had "caught up." The design of the chart is such that this improvement in osseous maturation is not immediately apparent.

very sensitive and shy, unable to get along well with children of his own age, and had both enuresis and encopresis.

Family History The mother was well, 5'4" tall, weighing 115 pounds. A brother age three and sister age two were of normal size. The father, 5'11" tall, had worked only occasionally, and living conditions for the family had always been inadequate and temporary. There were frequent violent disagreements between the parents, and the father was away from the home much of the time. The mother had been forced to support the family, occasionally holding two jobs at once, and thus was away from home during the day and often during most of the evening as well. During this time the patient was cared for by various relatives and "friends." The quality of care was frequently poor, and he was found to have "black and blue spots" on more than one occasion. At the time of this admission, the parents were separated, and the patient, with his mother and siblings, was living with the maternal grandmother.

Physical Findings This was an extremely small boy of six and one-half years who did not appear malnourished and was normally proportioned for his age (Fig. 2). His height was 99.8 cm. (height-age $3\frac{1}{2}$ years), his weight 12.9 kg., the upper segment/lower segment ratio 1.1, and his head circumference 47.5 centimeters. The blood pressure was 100/80 mm. of Hg. The skin color and temperature were normal, and the hair was fine. Dentition was normal for age. The chest and heart were normal. The abdomen was protuberant but otherwise normal. The genitalia were normal prepubertal male. The left leg was held in partial flexion and was 1.5 cm. longer than the right. The neurological examination was normal.

Laboratory Data Peripheral blood counts and urinalysis were normal. The cholesterol was 187 mg. per cent, and the I^{131} uptake 16 per cent in twenty-four hours. (More recently, the serum protein-bound iodine has been 7.5 and 5.5 micrograms per cent.) The blood non-protein nitrogen was 24 mg. per cent, the serum calcium 10.8 mg. per cent, the serum inorganic phosphorus 5.3 mg. per cent, and the alkaline phosphatase 15 Bodansky units. The fasting blood sugar was 88 mg. per cent.

Roentgenographic Findings   Films of the wrists showed a bone age of two and one-half years by Greulich-Pyle standards. X-ray studies of the upper gastrointestinal tract and intravenous pyelograms were normal. Studies of the hips, pelvis, and lower extremities were normal except for absence of the greater trochanter and fibular head centers, which should have appeared by four years of age.

Course   (Fig. 3) The boy was followed in this clinic through 1955, in which time he gained five cm. in height, and osseous maturation progressed to the three and one-half year level. During this period his mother was working and the boy lived with his grandmother. Enuresis and encopresis continued to be a problem, and school progress was poor. A Stanford-Binet score was 87 at this time. A trial of thyroid therapy during this time failed to affect growth or skeletal maturation significantly and was discontinued. He was not seen then for a two year period. During this time the mother had remarried and was able to stop working. Her new husband was an excellent provider, and was very kind to the children. The new home was quite comfortable. When next seen, in November 1957, at the age of ten years, ten months, his height was 123 cm., an increase of 18 cm., most of which had occurred in 1956, the preceding year. He seemed much more happy and outgoing than he had previously.

There was very early testicular enlargement (two x three cm.) but no other evidence of pubescence at this time, so that the growth spurt of the previous two years could hardly be ascribed to the hormonal changes of puberty. Bone age at this time was between five and six years. When seen one year later, he was 132 cm. in height, weighed 24 kg., and had advanced considerably in sexual maturation. The emotional problems persisted, however, still manifested by school failure, poor social adaptation, enuresis and encopresis. The boy and his parents were seen for an extended period by the child guidance clinic during 1958. Over the next two years, accelerated growth continued along with sexual maturation, bone age lagging considerably behind the other parameters of development. When last seen at the age of fourteen, however

(Fig. 4), skeletal age had accelerated and, with his height, now was near the 50th percentile for his actual age.

Case 5

History D.K., a twenty-two month old girl, was admitted to the Syracuse Memorial Hospital on October 5, 1960, for evaluation of her growth failure. She had been born prematurely, weighing 4 lbs. 4 oz. (1.9 kg.) at birth, and remained in the hospital nursery for twenty-three days. She was then said to have done well until the age of four months, when she became irritable and refused feedings. This made the mother "disgusted," and no further attempts were made to feed the child anything other than milk from a nursing bottle.

The family had been under the surveillance of the welfare department for several weeks prior to this. Neighbors had complained about the neglect of the older siblings, who were generally found to be hungry, dirty and poorly clad, and who were kept locked out of the house much of the time. The mother was reluctant to allow the case worker to see this child, who was found lying unclothed on a foam rubber mattress which was saturated with urine. She had a grayish pallor and her "ribs showed." She had an apathetic, "hopeless" cry, which had none of the vigor and anger of the cry of a normal hungry child. There was very little physical activity; she did not talk or sit without support. The mother seemed unconcerned about the child's condition, and asked that all the children be taken over by the welfare department.

Family History The mother, twenty-four, was well, and was separated from the father, who had a mild congenital hemiparesis. A paternal aunt, uncle, and grandmother also had this neurological syndrome. A brother, age five years, had spastic paraplegia secondary to perinatal anoxia. A sister, three, had athetoid cerebral palsy.

The mother lived with all of the children in a four room apartment, entirely supported by welfare assistance. She was described as being neatly dressed and of average intelligence, but seemed emotionless when discussing the children. She visited once while this child was in the hospital, and then only when requested to do so.

Physical Findings   This was a poorly developed and nourished, severely dwarfed girl of twenty-two months.   Her weight was 13 lbs. 3 oz. (6 kg.), and her body length 27 inches (67.5 cm.) (height-age 8 months).   Despite an alert facial expression, she did not talk. She was reluctant to sit, and did not pull up or stand (Fig. 13).   She exhibited frequent head-shaking and nodding, and often beat her head rhythmically against the bed for long periods of time.   Her skin was pale and dry, with pustular lesions in the diaper area. The head, eyes, ears, nose and throat were normal, as was her dentition.   The heart and chest were normal.   The abdomen was soft, with no masses or palpable organs.   The genitalia were nor-

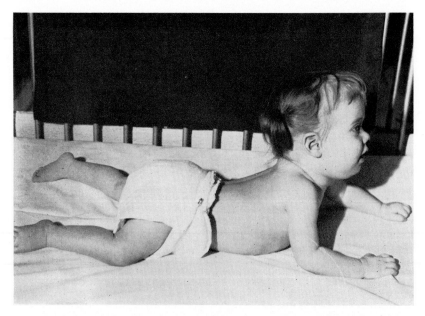

Fig. 13. Patient D.K. (Case 5) on admission to hospital for growth failure at age twenty-two months. She had a height-age of eight months. The infant showed rhythmic head-banging, nodding and shaking. She was poorly nourished, and made no effort to stand. At age four months the mother had become "disgusted" with the infant, and from then on only offered her whole milk from a nursing bottle.

mal. There were no neuromuscular abnormalities, other than the developmental retardation mentioned above.

Laboratory Data The hemoglobin was 9.3 gm. per cent, the hematocrit 33 per cent, the white blood cell count 9,500 per cubic mm., with 74 per cent lymphocytes. The red cells were moderately hypochromic. The urinalysis was normal. Stools were normal. The blood urea nitrogen was 10 mg. per cent. The sweat sodium was 43 meq. per liter, the chloride 46 meq. per liter. The alkaline phosphatase was 8.6 Bodansky units. The serum protein-bound iodine was 4.4 micrograms per cent, and 4.9 on a second determination. Muscle testing was normal in all groups.

Roentgenographic Findings The bone age was between three and six months by Greulich-Pyle standards.

Course There was an almost immediate response to hospitalization and to the personal attention given to the child by the nursing staff. Initially, her appetite was poor and no attempt was made to feed herself. Within a week, however, she was taking an active part in feeding, seemed to enjoy solid foods and was beginning to drink from a cup. Within a few days her withdrawn behavior had given way to obvious pleasure at being held and tended to by the nurses. After nine days on the ward, she was described as being "happy and alert." There was an acceleration of motor activity as well—she soon began to crawl, then to sit without support, to enjoy manipulating objects with her hands, to laugh and babble, and, three weeks after admission, to pull herself to a standing position (Fig. 14). On the thirty-first day, she walked without support, repeated several words. Her weight increased from 13 lbs. 3 oz. (6 kg.) to 17 lbs. 8 oz. (7.9 kg.) during her thirty-six day hospitalization, and body length increased one inch (2.5 cm.) over this same period. She was seen again three months after her discharge to a foster home. She was walking with support, saying many single words, and was said to be happy and responsive. At this time her height was 30 inches (75 cm.), her weight 24 lbs. 4 oz. (11 kg.), and her bone age was now at six to nine months by Greulich-Pyle standards (Figs. 15 and 16).

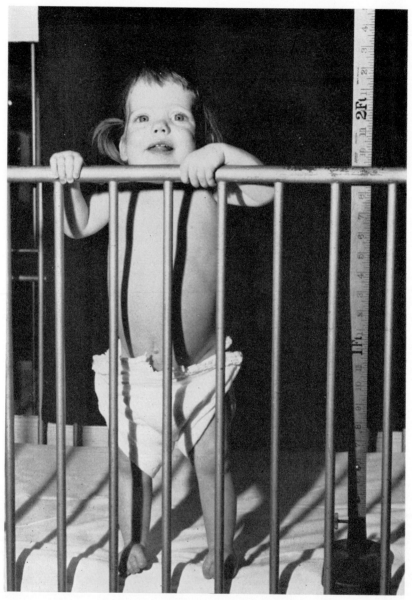

Fig. 14. Patient D.K. (Case 5) three weeks after hospital admission. Although her appetite was poor at first, within a week she had begun to respond to the attention of the nurses and was eating solid foods. By the third week, as the photograph shows, she was able to pull up to a standing position. She exhibited the "radar gaze" which has been observed in the recovery phase of maternal deprivation.

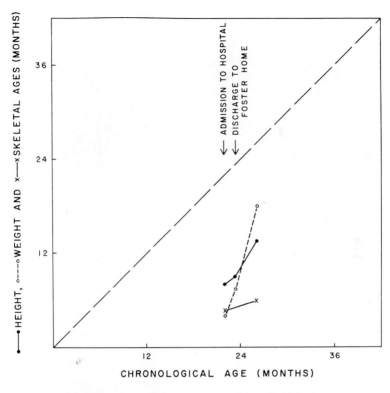

CASE 5 (D.K.)

Fig. 15. Growth chart of patient D.K. (Case 5). Note also in this case the "thin dwarf" pattern, with initial disproportionate retardation of weight-age (cf. Case 3, Fig. 12 and Case 2, Fig. 7). With improvement in her environment she gained weight rapidly, with her increment in body weight outstripping osseous maturation and linear growth. This phenomenon was also documented in Case 2, Figure 7.

Case 6

History R.W., an eighteen month old boy, was admitted to the Syracuse Memorial Hospital on January 9, 1961 for evaluation of poor growth and developmental retardation. He had been found by an investigating social worker, sitting alone on the bare floor of his poorly heated home, unresponsive to other people, and obviously suffering from physical neglect. He had been born at

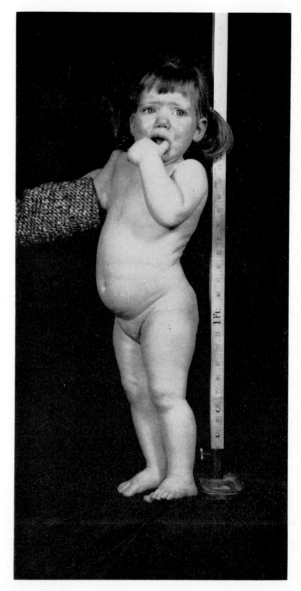

Fig. 16. Patient D.K. (Case 5) four months after hospitalization and three months after placement in a foster home. She is obviously no longer a "thin dwarf." She was walking with support, saying a number of words and happy and responsive.

term, following an uncomplicated pregnancy. There had been no immunizations or other medical care during infancy. His diet had consisted primarily of bread, with one or two glasses of "store milk" weekly and occasional meat. No vitamins had been given. He had been admitted to another hospital at one month of age for "bowel obstruction" but no surgery was done. Two months before this admission, the mother had spilled scalding water on his legs.

Family History The mother was in her mid-thirties. She was separated from the father, but another man was now living in the home. There were seven siblings, ranging in age from eleven years to three months. Three of these children were in foster homes. Another child had said that the mother and her "boy-friend" ate well, but that the children were left to go hungry.

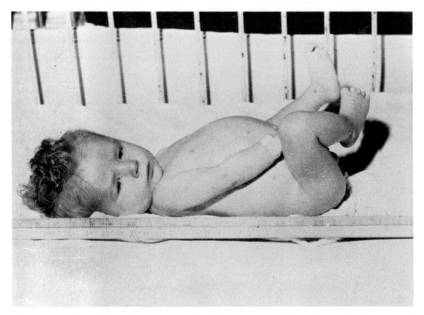

Fig. 17. Patient R.W. (Case 6) on admission at age eighteen months because of poor growth and development. His height-age was nine months and his bone age was twelve months. He had been found obviously suffering from physical neglect. He was unresponsive to other people and had a distant, wandering gaze.

Physical Findings This was a poorly developed boy of eighteen months, with a moderately distended abdomen, and thin extremities. He weighed 17 lbs. 2 ounces (7.7 kg.) and was 28 inches (70 cm.) in length (height-age 9 months). He was irritable and tried to avoid physical contact with people. He had a distant, wandering gaze, and was never seen to show recognition of people in his surroundings (Fig. 17). When disturbed, he began vigorous, rhythmic, rocking movements. Head rolling while supine was also seen frequently. He did not crawl, stand, or reach for objects. The head circumference was 18 inches (45 cm.), and the anterior fontanelle was one-half in. in diameter. There was pediculosis capitis. The eyes, ears, nose and throat were normal. Sixteen deciduous teeth were present. The chest was clear and the heart normal. There was slight flaring of the lower anterior rib cage. The abdomen was soft but distended. The liver and spleen were not enlarged. There was a right inguinal hernia. There was a "stocking and glove" erythema, with edema, of all distal extremities. There was a generalized excoriated maculopapular eruption, suggestive of insect bites. There was moderate enlargement of posterior cervical and inguinal lymph nodes. There were no detectable motor or sensory deficits, except for the retardation and behavior described above. There was generalized hyperreflexia, but no pathological reflexes.

Laboratory Data The hemoglobin was 11.1 gm. per cent, the hematocrit 37 per cent, the white blood cell count 9,600 per cubic mm. with a normal differential. The serum sodium was 135 meq. per liter and the potassium 3.6 meq. per liter. The serum calcium was 10.2 mg. per cent, and serum inorganic phosphorus 4.3 mg. per cent. The total serum proteins were 6.7 gm. per cent; the albumin 4.4, the globulin 2.3. The alkaline phosphatase was 3.3 Bessey-Lowry units. The urinalysis was normal. The blood urea nitrogen was 21.5 mg. per cent on admission. The fasting blood glucose was 88 mg. per cent. Stool cultures were normal (after an acute episode of diarrhea). A nose and throat culture grew pneumococci and beta-hemolytic streptococci. The serum protein-bound iodine was 6.7 micrograms per cent.

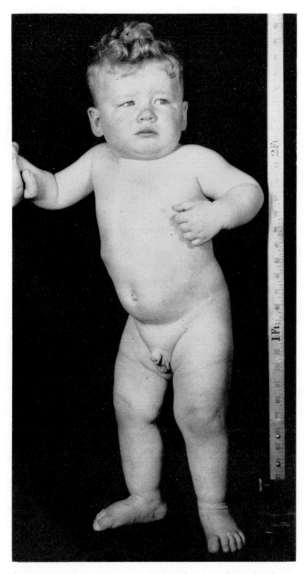

Fig. 18. Patient R.W. (Case 6) at age twenty-three and one-half months, having been with a foster mother for four and one-half months. He now appeared to be happy and well-adjusted. His nutrition had vastly improved, so that his weight-age exceeded his height-age, as seen previously in Case 2, Figure 7.

Roentgenographic Findings The bone age was twelve months. There was no x-ray evidence of rickets or scurvy. The chest film was normal, as was a barium enema, the latter being done because of the obstipation and abdominal distension.

Course There was little change in the withdrawn behavior during the first week, although a ravenous appetite and weight gain were immediate changes. The rhythmic rocking and head banging were noted frequently. During the third week, however, he began to show more interest in ward events, and on the twenty-first day, smiled, laughed, and seemed to enjoy playing with his nurse. He then began to respond to his name, and to play actively with toys. He reverted quickly to his withdrawn, rocking behavior when upset, however. He soon began to vocalize, enjoyed being up in his stroller, and was generally described as being cheerful and responsive. He was discharged to a foster home on the thirty-first day. His weight, on discharge, was 19 lbs., 8 oz. (8.8 kg.).

Within one month, he had gained 5 lbs. (2.4 kg.), was crawling and had begun to say a few single words. After three months he was pulling to a standing position and was "cruising." After four months, when twenty-three months of age, he first walked without assistance. When seen at this time he was robust and seemed happy. He showed close attachment to his foster mother, and smiled readily on appropriate stimulation. He weighed 30 lbs. 11 oz. (14.1 kg.) and was 30¾ inches (78 cm.) in height. His height-age was then sixteen months, and his "weight-age" thirty months, at an actual age of 23½ months (Fig. 18).

Chapter 5

> Mrs. W_____'s baby boy was puny, and his food didn't
> seem to agree with him. One day Dr. Balsley suggested that
> she turn the baby over to the care of her cook, Aunt Cindy.
> She did this, so the baby stayed in the kitchen and Aunt
> Cindy fed him like her own. Once Dr. Balsley went in to
> see him, and there he was, sitting happily in the middle of
> the kitchen floor, his face covered with grease, and a piece
> of fat-back in each hand. Soon he was well and strong, and
> he lived to be around seventy.
>
> BETTIE SUE GARDNER,
> *Eighty Years in Rockingham County,*
> Chap. 1, 1962

Summary and Conclusions

A syndrome of severe growth retardation, delayed skeletal maturation, and retarded psychomotor development has been found to be frequently associated with a specific disturbance of maternal behavior and family organization which has generally been termed "maternal deprivation." The deprivation has taken the form of rejection, isolation from social contacts, and neglect; physical abuse and malnutrition have been occasionally associated. Six such cases, each of whom was first brought to medical attention because of delayed growth or "failure to thrive," are described here. In each instance, the syndrome has developed while the child

81

has been living in the home with mother, although the clinical features seem to be almost identical with those previously described in institutionalized infants, and called "hospitalism" and "anaclitic depression" (20, 21).

Five of the children were first seen between the ages of thirteen and thirty-six months, the other one at six and one-half years. Height-ages ranged from 20 per cent to 65 per cent of the chronological ages, with a mean figure of 42 per cent. All of the five younger children were extremely underweight and appeared malnourished. Bone-ages were from 20 per cent to 67 per cent of the chronological ages, with a mean of 42 per cent. The bone-age/height-age ratios varied from 0.56 to 2.0, with a mean of 1.1. Dentition was normal for the actual ages.

There were no physical or laboratory findings which would have suggested the presence of specific endocrine or metabolic disorders, or of significant disease in any major organ system which might have been responsible for the growth retardation.

Other than the retardation in skeletal maturation, the only positive reoentgenologic findings were those of dense transverse lines at the ends of the long bones, and of osteoporosis in one case.

The five younger children (13-36 months) all were retarded developmentally. None was walking alone. Only the thirty-six month old child was talking, and he with a few unintelligible single words. All were extremely withdrawn, did not smile, and ignored surrounding objects or persons. Exaggerated rocking, head-banging, and other rhythmic motor activity was common. The one older boy was unable to establish normal relationships with his peers, and had enuresis and encopresis.

All of these children were products of grossly disturbed families, and were subjected to varying degrees of rejection, social isolation, or separation from mother, and in some cases to physical abuse and inadequate nutrition.

The oldest patient had an acceleration of growth which coincided in time with an improvement in the home situation. Among the five younger cases, there was a favorable response to hospitalization, with rapid weight gain, and with striking improvement in mood, social responsiveness, and in language and motor abilities.

These children were placed in supervised foster homes after the initial studies. This was done, however, only after repeated attempts by the courts and social agencies to attain satisfactory conditions for the children in their own homes, and it was hoped that this placement would be temporary in many cases. After an initial period of rapid amelioration, the long-term response in linear growth, weight gain, and skeletal maturation has been variable, with most of these parameters remaining below the 50th percentile for age during the periods of study. It is difficult to determine whether this "lag" is due to genetic factors, or to a permanent reduction in growth potential resulting from the unfavorable environmental circumstances of earlier childhood and infancy. Much the same can be said for the rate of improvement in affect, social behavior, and intellectual functions. The response to environmental change was initially quite favorable, with rapid improvement in these areas. The five younger patients, however, did not attain the developmental age norms during the periods of observation, and the two older patients, who have been followed into late childhood, show evidence of probable residual damage to personality structure and intellect.

The literature dealing with the behavioral and physiologic effects of infant deprivation is reviewed, and there is a discussion of the social factors which promote these effects in children. The various factors affecting the susceptibility of the child to deprivation are mentioned, and the development of current psychological theory relating to the mother-infant relationship is surveyed, with regard to animal experiments as well as clinical observations. There is then a review of clinical and experimental data related to the association of deprivation and emotional disorders with delay in somatic growth, followed by a discussion of those factors which possibly effect the reversibility of environmentally produced growth retardation. The significance of retarded skeletal maturation in this type of growth disturbance is discussed.

Conclusions

The close association of these disturbances of social and emotional environment with retardation of growth and development and a characteristic pattern of depressed and withdrawn behavior gives considerable support to the position that these environmental factors are of etiologic importance in this not uncommon syndrome, and that delay in growth and development may at times be a truly psychosomatic disorder. Lending additional support is the rapid and impressive early physical and behavioral response to the amelioration of the environmental circumstances. The failure to regain age norms completely in physical development, and the tendency to have residual defects in intellect and personality structure, however, suggest the existence of critical periods in the early phases of post-natal somatic growth and neural organization, during which unfavorable environmental factors may lead to an irreversible reduction in growth and developmental potential.

Whether this growth failure results from insufficient intake of calories, deficient intestinal absorption, or from direct hormonal or neurohumoral effects on cell metabolism, any effective approach to therapy must deal primarily with the underlying social and emotional disorders.

The prevention of infant deprivation can be discussed meaningfully only in relation to the socioeconomic and cultural characteristics of the society in which it occurs. The nature and magnitude of the problem are hardly the same in central Africa, for instance, where starvation and separation from parents are often the rule rather than the exception, and in the relatively stable and generally affluent population of an industrial city in the northeastern United States. As we have seen, these instances of deprivation, with their potentially disastrous effects on the future health and social and emotional adjustment of the affected children, seem to arise most frequently in families whose patterns of social maladjustment have been apparent in previous generations and seem to be self-perpetuating. As we have also said, there is not a direct relationship between the occurrence of maternal deprivation and economic status, and, in fact, the correct assessment of such situations may often require considerable perspicacity and diligence. Whether the primary causative factors are determined by environment or by inheritance, it does appear that deprivation begets deprivation, and that the solution to this problem lies in intelligent educational, social and political action toward breaking this cycle.

References

1. Rose, J. B. and McLaughlin, M. M.: *A Portable Medieval Reader.* New York, Viking Press, 1949.
2. Stone, L. J.: A critique of studies of infant isolation. *Child Development, 25*:9, 1954.
3. Benedek, T.: Psychological aspects of pregnancy and parent-child relationships. *Emotional Problems of Childhood,* edited by Samuel Liebman. Philadelphia, J. B. Lippincott Co., 1959.
4. Greulich, W. W. and Pyle, S. I.: *Radiographic Atlas of Skeletal Development of the Hand and Wrist,* Second Edition. Stanford University Press, 1959.
5. Snodgrasse, R. M., Dreizen, S., Currie, C., Parker, G. and Spies, T.: The association between anomalous ossification centers in the hand skeleton, nutritional status, and rate of skeletal maturation in children 5-14 years of age. *American Journal of Roentgenology, 74*:1037, 1955.
6. Dreizen, S., Stone, R. and Spies, T.: The influence of chronic undernutrition on bone growth in children. *Postgraduate Medicine, 29*:183, (Feb.) 1961.
7. Gesell, A. and Ilg, F.: *Infant and Child in the Culture of Today.* New York, Harper and Brothers, 1943.
8. Bowlby, J.: *Maternal Care and Mental Health.* World Health Organization Monograph Series. Geneva, 1952.
9. Brody, S.: *Patterns of Mothering.* New York, International Universities Press, 1956.
10. Hebb, D. O.: Sensory deprivation. *The American Psychologist, 13*:109, 1958.
11. Clarke, A. D. B. and Clarke, A. M.: Some recent advances in the study of early deprivation. *Child Psychology and Psychiatry, 1*:26, 1960.
12. Dennis, W.: Infant development under conditions of restricted practice and of minimum social stimulation. *Genetic Psychology Monographs, 23*:143, 1941.
13. Gesell, A. and Amatruda, T.: *Developmental Diagnosis.* New York, Paul B. Hoeber, Inc., 1941.
14. Sprague, J. M., Chambers, W. W. and Stellar, E.: Attentive, affective, and adaptive behavior in the cat. *Science, 133*:165, (Jan. 20) 1961.
15. Lowrey, L. G.: Personality distortion and early institutional care. *The American Journal of Orthopsychiatry, 10*:576, (July) 1940.

16. Goldfarb, W.: Effects of psychological deprivation in infancy and subsequent stimulation. *American Journal of Psychiatry, 102*: 18, 1945.

17. Goldfarb, W.: Psychological privation in infancy and subsequent adjustment. *The American Journal of Orthopsychiatry, 15*:247, 1945.

18. Richmond, J. B. and Hersher, L.: Personal communication.

19. Freedman, D., King, J. and Elliot, O.: Critical period in the social development of dogs. *Science, 133*:1016, (March 31) 1961.

20. Spitz, R. A.: Hospitalism. *The Psychoanalytic Study of the Child, II*:113, 1946.

21. Spitz, R. A. and Wolff, K.: Anaclitic depression. *The Psychoanalytic Study of the Child, II*:313, 1946.

22. Ripin, R.: A comparative study of the development of infants in an institution with those in homes of low socioeconomic status. *Psychological Bulletin, 30*:860, 1933.

23. Goldfarb, W.: The effects of early institutional care on adolescent personality. *Journal of Experimental Education, 12*:106, 1943.

24. Bakwin, H.: Loneliness in infants. *American Journal of Diseases in Children, 63*:30, (Jan.) 1942.

25. Bakwin, H.: Emotional deprivation in infants. *Journal of Pediatrics, 35*:512, (Oct.) 1949.

26. Ribble, M.: Infantile experience in relation to personality development. *Personality and the Behavior Disorders*, edited by J. McV. Hunt. New York, Ronald, 1944.

27. Tanner, J. M.: *Growth at Adolescence.* Springfield, Thomas, 1955.

28. Låt, J., Widdowson, E. M. and McCance, R. A.: Some effects of accelerating growth. III. Behavior and nervous activity. *Proceedings of the Royal Society, B, 153*:347, 1960.

29. Engel, G. L. and Reichsman, F.: Spontaneous and experimentally induced depressions in an infant with a gastric fistula—a contribution to the problem of depression. *Journal of the American Psychoanalytic Association, 4*:428, (July) 1956.

30. Coleman, R. and Provence, S.: Developmental retardation (hospitalism) in infants living in families. *Pediatrics, 19*:285, 1957.

31. Elmer, E.: Failure to thrive—role of the mother. *Pediatrics, 25*: 717, (April) 1960.

32. Darwin, C.: A biographical sketch of an infant. *Mind, 7*:285, (July) 1877.

33. Bowlby, J.: The nature of a child's tie to his mother. *The International Journal of Psychoanalysis, 39*:350, 1958.

34. Benedek, T.: The psychosomatic implications of the primary unit; mother-child. *American Journal of Orthopsychiatry, 19*:642, (Oct.) 1949.

35. Ribble, M.: *The Rights of Infants.* New York, Columbia University Press, 1943.

36. Harlow, H. F.: The nature of love. *The American Psychologist, 13*:673, (Dec.) 1958.

37. Harlow, H. F. and Zimmerman, R.: Affectional responses in the infant monkey. *Science, 130*:421, (August 21) 1959.

38. Harlow, H. F.: The maternal and infantile affectional patterns. Salmon Lecture 2.

39. Engel, L.: The troubled monkeys of Madison. *The New York Times Magazine,* p. 62, Jan. 29, 1961.

40. Brazelton, T. B.: Psychophysiologic reactions in the neonate. I. The value of observation of the neonate. *The Journal of Pediatrics, 58*:508, (April) 1961.

41. Clements, F.: Nutrition in maternal and infant feeding. Proceedings of the 5th International Congress of Nutrition. *Federation Proceedings, 20*: Part III, Supplement 7, p. 165, 1961.

42. Jelliffe, D. B. and Bennett, F. J.: Cultural and anthropological factors in infant and maternal nutrition. Proceedings of the 5th International Cong. of Nutrition. *Federation Proceedings, 20*: Suppl. 7, p. 185, 1961.

43. Geber, M. and Dean, R. F. A.: Psychological factors in the etiology of Kwashiorkor. *W.H.O. Bulletin, 12*:471, 1955.

44. Beaumont, William: *Experiments and Observations on the Gastric Juice and the Physiology of Digestion.* Plattsburg, F. P. Allen, 1833.

45. Engel, G. L., Reichsman, F. and Segal, H.: A study of an infant with gastric fistula. I. Behavior and the rate of total HCl secretion. *Psychosomatic Medicine, 18*:374, (Sept.-Oct.) 1956.

46. Jordan, W. K. and Merritt, H. H.: Medical progress—neurology. *The New England Journal of Medicine, 260*:644, (Mar. 26) 1959.

47. Harris, G. W.: Central nervous system control of gonadotropic and thyrotropic secretion. *Advance Abstracts of Symposium Lectures and Round Table Discussion.* 1st International Congress of Endocrinology, p. 15. Copenhagen, Periodica, 1960.

48. Reichlin, S.: Thyroid function, body temperature regulation and growth in rats with hypothalamic lesions. *Endocrinology, 66:* 340, (March) 1960.

49. Jordan, W. K. and Merritt, H. H.: Medical progress—neurology. *The New England Journal of Medicine, 255:*468, (Sept. 6) 1956.

50. Bogdonoff, M. and Estes, E. H.: Energy dynamics and acute states of arousal in man. *Psychosomatic Medicine, 23:*23, (Jan.-Feb.) 1961.

51. Reichlin, S.: Growth and the hypothalamus. *Endocrinology, 67:* 760, 1960.

52. Talbot, N. B., Sobel, E. H., Burke, B., Lindemann, E. and Kaufman, S.: Dwarfism in healthy children: its possible relation to emotional, nutritional and endocrine disturbances. *New England Journal of Medicine, 236:*783, (May 22) 1947.

53. Fried, R. and Mayer, M. F.: Socioemotional factors accounting for growth failure in children living in an institution. *Journal of Pediatrics, 33:*444, 1948.

54. Binning, G.: "Peace be on thy house"—the effects of emotional tensions on the development and growth of children, based on a study of 800 Saskatoon school children. *Health.* Toronto, March-April, 1948.

55. Widdowson, E. M.: Mental contentment and physical growth. *Lancet, 1:*1316, (June 16) 1951.

56. Bransby, E. R., Burn, J. L., Magee, H. E. and MacKecknie, D. M.: Effect of certain social conditions on the health of school children. *British Medical Journal, 2:*767, 1946.

57. Wolff, G.: Increased bodily growth of school children since the war. *Lancet, 1:*1006, (April 27) 1935.

58. Aron, H.: Wachstum und Ernährung. *Biochimische Zeitschrift, 30:*207, 1911.

59. Osborne, T. B. and Mendel, L. B.: The suppression of growth and the capacity to grow. *Journal of Biological Chemistry, 18:*95, 1914.

60. Jackson, C. M.: Recovery of rats upon refeeding after prolonged suppression of growth by underfeeding. *The Anatomical Record, 68:*371, (June) 1937.

61. Clarke, M. F. and Smith, A. H.: Recovery following suppression of growth in the rat. *Journal of Nutrition, 15:*245, (March) 1938.

62. Barnes, L. L., Sperling, G. and McCay, C. M.: Bone growth in normal and retarded growth rats. *Journal of Gerontology, 2*: 240, (July) 1947.

63. Saxton, J. C. and Silberberg, M.: Skeletal growth and aging in rats receiving complete or restricted diets. *American Journal of Anatomy, 81*:445, (Nov.) 1947.

64. Widdowson, E. M. and McCance, R. A.: Some effects of accelerating growth. I. General somatic development. *Proceedings of the Royal Society, B, 152*:188, 1960.

65. Kennedy, G. C.: The development with age of hypothalamic restraint upon the appetite of the rat. *Journal of Endocrinology, 16*:9, (Nov.) 1957.

66. McCay, C. M., in Cowdry's *Problems of Ageing*. Baltimore, Williams and Wilkins, 1952, p. 139.

67. Mellman, W. J., Bongiovanni, A. M. and Hope, J. W.: The diagnostic usefulness of skeletal maturation in an endocrine clinic. *Pediatrics, 23*:530, (Mar.) 1959.

68. Francis, C.: Factors influencing appearance of centers of ossification during early childhood. *American Journal of Diseases of Children, 59*:1006, (May) 1940.

69. Gopalan, C.: Kwashiorkor in Uganda and Coonoor. *Journal of Tropical Pediatrics, 1*:206, 1955.

70. Jones, P. R. M. and Dean, R. F. A.: The effects of Kwashiorkor on the development of the bones of the knee. *Journal of Pediatrics, 54*:176, 1959.

71. Dickerson, J. W. T. and Widdowson, E. M.: Some effects of accelerating growth. II. Skeletal development. *Proceedings of the Royal Society, B, 152*:207, 1960.

72. Nissen, H. W. and Riesen, A. H.: Retardation in onset of ossification in chimpanzee related to various environmental and physiologic factors. *The Anatomical Record, 105*:655, (Dec.) 1949.

73. Caffey, J.: *Pediatric X-ray Diagnosis*. Chicago, The Year Book Publishers, 1945.

INDEX*

A

Allee, W. C., 11r
Amatruda, T., 32, 85r
Amsel, A., 5, 11r
amygdaloid nuclei, 43
"anaclitic depression," 9, 16, 43, 82
anorexia, in adults with experimental
    isolation, 10
Aron, H., 46, 88r
"autism," experimental, in cats produced
    by sectioning lemnisci in midbrain,
    32
"autistic" behavior (case 6), 28
autonomic centers, 44

B

Bakwin, H., 34, 86r
Barnes, L. L., 47, 89r
Beaumont, William, 42, 87r
Benedek, T., 39, 41, 85r, 87r
Benjamin, J. D., 12r
Bernstein, L., 12r
Binning, G., 45, 88r
Bly, C. G., 12r
Bogdonoff, M., 88r
bone age
    retardation, analysis of causes, 49
    control by endocrine system, 49
Bongiovanni, A. M., 89r
Bovard, E. W., 12r
Bowlby, J., 32, 40, 85r, 87r

Bransby, E. R., 45, 88r
Brattgard, S., 4, 11r
Brazelton, T. B., 41, 87r
Brewer, N. R., 11r
Brody, S., 31, 85r
Burke, B., 88r
Burn, J. L., 88r

C

Caffey, J., 50, 89r
Candland, D. R., 13r
case histories, 52 *et seq*.
Casler, L., 11, 13r
Chambers, W. W., 85r
chimpanzees
    darkness and delayed ossseous matura-
        tion, 5
    retarded bone-age associated with light
        deprivation, 50
Clarke, A. D. B., 34, 37, 85r
Clarke, A. M., 34, 37, 85r
Clarke, M. F., 47, 88r
Clements, F., 87r
"cold injury," in maternal deprivation, 27
Coleman, R., 36, 86r
Currie, C., 85r

D

Darwin, Charles, atavistic concept of
    infant behavior, 39, 86r
Dean, R. F. A., 42, 50, 87r, 89r
Dennis, W., 85r

---

*A lower case "r" after a page number indicates that item occurs in a bibliographic reference.

91